OPPORTUNITIES

in

Pharmacy Careers

REVISED EDITION

FRED B. GABLE

VGM Career Books

Chicago   New York   San Francisco   Lisbon   London   Madrid   Mexico City
Milan   New Delhi   San Juan   Seoul   Singapore   Sydney   Toronto

The **McGraw·Hill** Companies

Library of Congress Cataloging-in-Publication Data

Gable, Fred B.
    Opportunities in pharmacy careers / Fred B. Gable — Rev. ed.
        p.   cm. (VGM opportunities series)
    ISBN 0-07-141152-6
    1. Pharmacy—Vocational guidance.   2. Pharmacy—Vocational guidance—
United States.   I. Title.   II. Series.

    RS122.5.G3   2004
    615'.1'023—dc21   2003056396

1 2 3 4 5 6 7 8 9 0   LBM/LBM   2 1 0 9 8 7 6 5 4 3

ISBN 0-07-141152-6

Interior design by Rattray Design

McGraw-Hill books are available at special quantity discounts to use as premiums and sales promotions, or for use in corporate training programs. For more information, please write to the Director of Special Sales, Professional Publishing, McGraw-Hill, Two Penn Plaza, New York, NY 10121-2298. Or contact your local bookstore.

This book is printed on acid-free paper.

In memory of my mother and father, who encouraged me
to become what I wanted to become

Contents

Pharmacy as a career. Pharmacy: a definition. Pharmacy manpower. Pharmacy's history: galenicals to gene therapy.

Education in flux. Organizational name changes. FDA pace quickens. Industrial merger mania. Chain pharmacy takeovers. Health-care innovations. A bright future.

The growth of pharmaceutical education. Battle of the degrees. High school highlights. Early admission

programs. Standard tests for high school students.
Prepharmacy college requirements. Exceptions and
variations. Pharm.D.1 and Pharm.D.2 degrees.

Administration and management. Pharmacy aides and
pharmacy technicians. Health information center. The
pharmacist: a permanent student. Specialized practices.
Pharmacy practice incentives.

Foreword

As OUR NATION's health-care system evolves to meet the challenges of a growing and varied population, the profession of pharmacy offers its practitioners unparalleled opportunities to develop skills, interests, and new career paths both in and outside of the health-care field.

A brief look at the morning newspaper or a quick scan of the Internet confirms that our world is rapidly changing and creating new demands for health-care professionals who can understand the innovative intricacies of care. Shorter hospital stays, an emphasis on home care, and changing ways to treat diseases and illnesses are just a few of the developments that are redefining American health care and making the pharmacist a pivotal member of the health-care team.

The profession of pharmacy is unfolding not only in the way that pharmacy services are provided but, more importantly, in the kinds of services that are provided. No longer do pharmacists simply dispense medications. Working under collaborative practice agree-

ments with physicians and other prescribers, today's pharmacist takes an active role in monitoring patient medication therapy and goes into the community to conduct specific patient-care programs such as cholesterol monitoring and immunizations for children and seniors.

Although many pharmacists continue to practice in community pharmacies, the traditional practice sites are changing. Pharmacists are indispensable members of every health-care setting. They practice in hospitals and in managed-care centers, they work with physicians to treat patients, and they offer online pharmaceutical care.

It's not easy to become a pharmacist. Most university programs leading to the doctor of pharmacy degree require six years to complete. But if you have an interest in the health-care field and a desire to make a difference in patients' lives, the profession of pharmacy will provide the challenges and rewards you seek. As you begin to consider your future career goals, I hope you will take the time to review *Opportunities in Pharmacy Careers.*

Carmen A. Catizone
Executive Director/Secretary
National Association of Boards of Pharmacy

Preface

THERE'S SOMETHING ABOUT pharmacists. They're gentle, bright, versatile, caring, honest, dedicated, flexible, tough, nimble, generous, kind, intelligent, and likable. Consumers have long had affection and respect for the neighborhood druggist, who was commonly addressed as "Doc" decades and decades before the doctor of pharmacy degree ever crossed anyone's mind as the entitled and ultimate degree now awarded to a new generation of pharmacy graduates.

Replying to a junior high school teacher whose students wanted to know which occupations commanded the most respect, advisory columnist Ann Landers published the results of a Gallup Poll that asked fifteen hundred people across the United States how they rated "honesty and ethical standards" of workers in twenty-four varied career choices: very high, high, average, low, or very low. For careers ranked very high/high for honesty and ethical standards, clergy placed first with 63 percent of respondents, and pharmacists ranked second with 59 percent! College teachers came in sixth with a score of 45 percent, and senators ranked fourteenth with a score of 21 percent.

The pharmacist in 1950 knew all that was known about drugs at that time in history, just as today's pharmacist is recognized and acknowledged first and foremost as the drug expert. In 1950, consumers knew the reliable and dependable pharmacist could remove an eye cinder, bandage an injured finger, soothe a rash, and ease sunburn. It's impossible to describe the kaleidoscope of pharmaceutical care that is offered today by pharmacists across the country. No single pharmacist does it all, but individual pharmacists have fortes that are sparked by unique motivations and interests coupled with the desire to meet general and specific health needs of a community.

In 1994, for the first time, nearly two thousand Walgreens pharmacies offered flu shots to the elderly and infirm for a nominal fee of ten dollars. Some pharmacists have successfully developed home monitoring programs for hypertensive patients. With the encouragement of physicians, pharmacists working with diabetics now instruct patients in the use of blood glucose monitors as well as how to interpret results. A Boston pharmacist who received a grant for practitioner innovation in pharmaceutical care from the American Pharmaceutical Association has built a following related to counseling attention deficit disorder (ADD) patients through recommendation of drugs, monitoring of side effects, and evaluation of patient lifestyles.

The face of pharmacy is in flux as legislators, educators, practitioners, and administrators mull the alternatives of professional practice that are open to the men and women engaged in the prodigious and multifaceted profession of pharmacy. With me, on the pages that follow, visit the spaces of pharmacy now open to pharmacists throughout the country. Welcome to the world of pharmacy!

ACKNOWLEDGMENTS

THE AUTHOR WISHES to thank the following individuals and their organizations: Daniel A. Nona, Executive Director, American Council on Pharmaceutical Education, Chicago; Sandra Kay Jung, Manager, Professional Services and Programs, National Association of Chain Drug Stores, Alexandria, Virginia; Carmen A. Catizone, Executive Director/Secretary, National Association of Boards of Pharmacy, Park Ridge, Illinois; Raymond Bounds, Jr., R.Ph., Veterans Administration, Ambulatory Care Center, Philadelphia; Rear Admiral Fred G. Paavola, R.Ph., Chief Pharmacist Officer, United States Public Health Service, Rockville, Maryland; John A. Gans, Pharm.D., Executive Vice President, American Pharmaceutical Association, Washington, D.C.; Charles M. Dragovich, Pharmacist, Associate Director of Student Affairs, American Pharmaceutical Association, Washington, D.C.; Sylvia Robinson, R.Ph.,

Independent Pharmacy Owner, Samuel J. Robinson Pharmacy, Philadelphia.

Special appreciation goes to the administrators of the American Association of Colleges of Pharmacy (AACP) and the Pharmaceutical Research and Manufacturers of America (PhRMA) for their celerity and cooperation in providing the invaluable information and statistics that enhanced and augmented this writing.

1

An Overview: The Evolution of Pharmacy

Everyone is ultimately confronted with the important decision of selecting a means of earning a living. There are those fortunate individuals who are inspired at an early age to pursue a particular career and never waver in their quest until the objective is attained. The youth who chooses a career in his or her teens and follows an unfaltering path toward goal achievement is the exception rather than the rule. Many college students move in and out of various curricula in search of gratification, and increasing numbers of working adults return to college in preparation for newly found goals.

Uncertainty in making a career choice should not disturb the seeker. However, considerable time and energy must be devoted to this important decision. Its outcome will determine how one spends at least forty years—or eighty thousand working hours—of a lifetime. Errors in judgment can be minimized through intense investigation of potential occupations.

Pharmacy as a Career

If you believe that pharmacy is a good career choice for you, there are a number of things you can do to find out about the field and what you have to do to become a functioning and productive member of it.

Counselors

Guidance counselors in secondary schools, community colleges, and liberal arts institutions are resourceful individuals whose assistance should be sought initially. Counselors will provide oral and written information about specific careers and lists of schools in the chosen field. The skilled counselor may also help one establish guidelines for the sort of work that is suitable given the individual's innate capacity, interest, and/or readiness in learning. Students owe it to themselves to follow up on information offered by the counselor. This is accomplished by writing to recommended schools for literature and by visiting public and school libraries for additional reading material about the career under consideration.

Contact with Pharmacists

Often overlooked as obvious sources of information are people working in the desired field. An aspiring pharmacist would do well to speak with men and women practicing pharmacy in community and institutional settings. A behind-the-scenes visit to a community pharmacy will be very enlightening to one considering this career. Ask the pharmacist in charge to discuss the advantages and disadvantages inherent in the profession. Everyone has a community pharmacy nearby, but it is best to consult the pharmacist as to

the most convenient time for a meeting to review career aspects. A phone call to the nearest hospital will put you in touch with the person in charge of the pharmacy. Once you explain the nature of your call, it should result in an invitation to meet with the pharmacist and observe the operation of this important unit within the hospital. Remember to review the occupations of neighbors, friends, relatives, and their acquaintances to avoid overlooking excellent information sources.

Do not terminate this person-to-person survey following one or two meetings. Surprisingly different insights will be obtained from each contact, and the more professionals you encounter, the better you will understand the true nature of the field. Prior to meeting with someone in your field of interest, be certain to do your homework by reading as much as possible about the career. Such advance knowledge will permit you to establish rapport with the professional and better understand the information provided during the exchange. Afterward, you should also write to those with whom you met and thank them for their valuable assistance. In years to come, it is possible that these same individuals may be considering you in your search for employment!

Ability and Motivation

One inevitably asks oneself, "How can I tell if I'm the kind of person to become a professional in my chosen field?" Two factors having the greatest influence upon the answer are ability and motivation. Ability may be ascertained to some extent by evaluating the grades on the high school transcript. This is not always a valid tool because there are those students who, for various reasons, do not fully apply themselves during secondary school. Some devote too

much time and energy to extracurricular programs in athletics, drama, or newspaper or yearbook writing projects, thereby neglecting regularly scheduled classes. Of course, the benefits of extracurricular activities to physical and social development are significant, but these are not always reflected on a transcript. Some encounter physical or mental illness that interferes with attendance and academic performance. Some, due to financial necessity, are working during nonschool hours and lack the time to study and complete homework. Others simply fail to recognize the importance of achieving a good academic record because they lack motivation toward a particular objective.

Motivation is an intangible quality that prompts a person to act in a certain way, and, therefore, it is difficult to measure. Psychologists and sociologists remain concerned with the socialization process that endows one with the ideals, values, attitudes, and ambitions that provide a unique sense of identity. Many believe the motivation of an individual is determined by countless childhood experiences and influences. Parents, home environment, neighbors, schools, and birthplace all contribute to the socialization process. Dramatic innovations in transportation, communication, education, health care, and lifestyle have had a profound effect on society. In addition, thanks to technology, an imposing array of career choices adds to the complexity of deciding on an occupation.

Interest in the Profession

What attracts one to a career in pharmacy? A personal relationship with a pharmacist directs some toward this career. Pharmacists are as visible as goldfish in a bowl as they practice their profession in the open, encountering hundreds of clients every day. The sights and smells of the community pharmacy stimulate interest in the profession, and many clerks and delivery personnel develop profes-

sional aspirations through entry-level job associations. College representatives visiting high schools for career conferences may also plant the seed of interest in pharmacy. Widespread public interest in drugs and their usage, as evidenced by newspaper, magazine, and television coverage, may serve as the entrée to pharmacy. Personal experiences of illness within a family have alerted some to the wonders of drugs and the role of the pharmacist on the health delivery team. Some may be attracted to pharmacy because of the excellent salaries that pharmacists command. Needless to say, the reasons different people become pharmacists are diverse and multifaceted.

The man or woman interested in science, health, working and communicating with people, serving the community, and contributing to public service would do well to consider pharmacy as a career. These are the personal qualifications that provide the motivation to become a professional in the field of pharmacy.

Humanistic relationships remain at the core of pharmacy practice. Thus the pharmacist, though a drug expert, must have a strong interest and concern for human values and dignity. Reflect on your incentive for pharmacy before reckoning with the scholastic aspects of the situation. The strongly motivated student with average grades will make a better practicing pharmacist than the apathetic student with outstanding grades. Students who ranked at the bottom of their high school class have the opportunity to demonstrate their scholastic abilities during the first year in a community college or liberal arts institution. The desire to achieve is all-important. If you have the desire and interest to become a pharmacist, read on!

Pharmacy: A Definition

Pharmacy is a health profession concerned specifically with the knowledge of drugs and wisdom in their use. A definition should

precisely encompass the meaning of a word and provide fixed limits that prevent vagueness or generality. The definition of pharmacy as presented lacks such limits because the expansiveness of modern pharmacy defies confinement. Fifty years ago one could state with authority, as *Webster's* did, that the "primary function of pharmacy is to prepare medicines for those who require them." Even today a current dictionary inaccurately defines pharmacy as "the art and science of preparing and dispensing drugs." These outmoded definitions take into account only the drug-delivery aspects of the field and ignore the current role of the pharmacist as a health-system provider who is sensitive to the needs of patients. In defense of harried lexicographers who must update meanings of many words, it should be noted that even pharmacists have difficulty keeping abreast of countless legislative, scientific, economic, social, and professional forces that incessantly alter the face of pharmacy.

It is harder to define *pharmacist* than it is to define *pharmacy*. One may begin by describing a pharmacist as a graduate of an accredited school of pharmacy who is actively employed within some phase of the profession. Pharmacists perform their tasks in various settings. White-coated community pharmacists are the most visible because they represent the greatest number of participants within the profession and perform their services in neighborhood pharmacies. Institutional pharmacists are also white-coated practitioners, but they are less visible because they work in hospitals, clinics, and nursing homes. Both community and institutional pharmacists are dedicated to pharmacy practice, which the American Pharmaceutical Association defines as "a patient-oriented health service that applies a scientific body of knowledge to improve and promote health through assurances of safety and effectiveness in drug use and drug-related therapy."

Specialty Areas

Thousands of other pharmacists are employed in specialty areas that do not involve patients or drug-delivery aspects. Specialization is a process of division that occurs when knowledge and assignments within a discipline increase to such an extent that it becomes unfeasible for practitioners to master all of that discipline's branches. Specialization has affected many fields as their banks of knowledge increase in content and complexity. Advancements in the science of chemistry, for example, have led to the training of chemists in organic chemistry, analytical chemistry, physical chemistry, biochemistry, colloidal chemistry, medicinal chemistry, pharmaceutical chemistry, and other specialties. Prior to specialization, the medical profession consisted primarily of general practitioners who set bones, delivered babies, and treated any disease or disorder that troubled the patient. Today medical doctors study various specialties to become rhinologists (dealing with the nose), ophthalmologists (eyes), otologists (ears), gynecologists (women's health), pediatricians (children), dermatologists (skin), obstetricians (childbirth), orthopedists (spine), neurologists (nervous system), and psychiatrists (mental illness), to mention just some of the branches of medicine.

Specialization within health professions has developed to an amazing extent, and the public has benefited by obtaining superior services and improvements in everyday life. A vast number of specialists in medicine, nursing, dentistry, and pharmacy work together toward a common goal—the improvement of public health. Doctors, dentists, nurses, and pharmacists are members of a health-care delivery team, working cooperatively in the battle to preserve health and prevent disease. The health science team in the United States

has a most impressive record as evidenced by statistics. People born at the turn of the twentieth century had a life expectancy of 49.2 years. Today the average American born in 1994 can expect to live more than 75 years, and life expectancy has risen dramatically for all age groups. Every four years since 1965, one additional year has been added to life expectancy at birth.

The profession of pharmacy has made significant contributions to the advancement of public health in the United States, and specialization has played an important role. Some men and women with pharmacy degrees pursue careers in the pharmaceutical industry, pharmacy teaching, pharmacy research, pharmacy administration, pharmaceutical sales, and other specialty areas. Such pharmacists are not easily recognized as they utilize pharmaceutical backgrounds while executing special skills in their jobs. Those in industry may work in laboratories or offices, garbed respectively in long protective laboratory smocks or ordinary street dress. Pharmacy professors dress casually while teaching students in schools of pharmacy and then switch to lab coats when duties take them from lecture rooms to laboratories. The pharmaceutical salesperson dresses smartly as he or she visits physicians to inform them of new drugs available for patient use. Extensive information about these specialties and others in pharmacy will be presented in forthcoming chapters.

Pharmacy Manpower

Manpower refers to the number of people employed simultaneously at the same job within a geographical area. In pharmacy, the subject of manpower unequivocally includes woman-power, for women comprise a significant segment of the profession. Surveys revealed that in 2000 approximately 46 percent of all pharmacists

in the United States were women. This percentage will continue to increase because during recent decades there has been dramatic growth in women's enrollment in pharmacy schools. In academic year 2000–2001, women accounted for 66.3 percent of the total enrollment in schools of pharmacy in the United States. Beginning in 1982, the collective enrollment of women in all schools of pharmacy in the United States exceeded 50 percent (51.9 percent) for the first time. In 1995 the collective enrollment of women in all seventy-nine schools of pharmacy reached a peak of 63.4 percent. In 2001, graduates of pharmacy schools (now totaling eighty-three) in the United States consisted of 64.5 percent female pharmacists (statistics from the American Association of Colleges of Pharmacy). These pharmacy statistics confirm the overall picture of women in the American workplace as presented in a report, "Women, Work, and Family in America," published in January 1997 by the nonprofit Population Reference Bureau. This independent summary noted that between 1970 and 1995, the share of women age twenty-five to fifty-four employed outside the home climbed from 50 percent to 76 percent, with the biggest gains shown by married women with children.

The most recent report of the Bureau of Labor Statistics (*Occupational Outlook Handbook, 2002–03*) estimates there are 217,000 people in this country who are licensed for pharmacy practice. Of the total number, approximately 85 percent are actively engaged in pharmacy practice or specialty practice within the profession (about 21 percent of salaried pharmacists work in hospitals, clinics, mail-order pharmacies, pharmaceutical wholesaler companies, home health-care agencies, and for the federal government). Thus 15 percent of those eligible to participate do not do so because they are retired or ill, are engaged as homemakers managing a home and/or raising young children, or have entered other professions such as

primary or secondary school teaching, medicine, dentistry, podiatry, or law through additional collegiate studies while registered as pharmacists.

Manpower in the health professions may be expressed as a rate by calculating the number of professionals per 1,000. Utilizing data from the Bureau of Labor Statistics, in the year 2000 there were 2,200 nurses, 598 physicians and surgeons, 217 pharmacists, 152 dentists, 59 veterinarians, 31 optometrists, and 18 podiatrists per 1,000 people in the health professions.

It is difficult to project if health professionals will be in short supply in 2020 or if the anticipated numbers of professionals will exceed the demand for service. Some demographers believe there will be a favorable balance between health practitioners and population. Others point out that geographic inequities will persist into the twenty-first century, and some health professionals will be forced to relocate to parts of the United States where medical care is scarce. Sometimes overlooked is the fact that while our population may not increase rapidly, the proportion of older people increased from 4 percent in 1900 to 13 percent in 1996, and this 13 percent segment of the population accounts for roughly 34 percent of health expenditures. By the year 2020, an estimated 25 percent of the nation's population, more than sixty-five million Americans, will be at least sixty-five years of age.

According to the *Occupational Outlook Handbook, 2002–03*, employment of pharmacists is expected to grow as fast as the average for all occupations (10 to 20 percent) through the year 2010 due to the increased pharmaceutical needs of a larger and older population and greater use of medications. The growing numbers of middle-aged and elderly people—who, on average, use more prescription drugs than do younger people—will continue to spur demand for pharmacists in all practice settings.

Other factors likely to increase demand for pharmacists include scientific advances that will make more drug products available, new developments in genome research and distribution systems, and increasingly sophisticated consumers seeking more information about drugs.

In fact, a shortage of pharmacists may occur by the year 2005 due to economic and demographic factors (such as the impact of an older population) that cannot wholly be foreseen today. Predicting future trends in pharmacy is a challenge because of the great number of uncertainties and variables that will ultimately pattern the practice of this ancient profession. A look at the evolution of pharmacy will provide the future pharmacist with a sense of the esprit de corps enjoyed by members of a long-standing and proud profession.

Pharmacy's History: Galenicals to Gene Therapy

Self-preservation is an instinct characteristic of mankind. Prehistoric men and women were just as concerned about survival against diseases and disorders as are people living in an age of space travel. Those who lived centuries ago used all known means in their battle to preserve health just as we do today. Those who are sick are afflicted with ill health or disease that forces them to live differently from what is customary. A universal quality of all who are ill is the desire to return to normalcy. When one is ill, the rhythm of existence is broken by symptoms of uneasiness and discomfort that may include fever, insomnia, pain, appetite loss, or other indications that something is not right. Today's modern method of dealing with sickness is a far cry from the mysticism and sorcery that prevailed in the healing arts of bygone cultures and civilizations.

The earliest records of medical and pharmaceutical practices date to the Egyptian era during the reign of Cheops, King of Egypt. Records of written prescriptions appear on stone tablets dating back to 3600 B.C. Serpents were commonly used in healing rituals, and the sick prayed to snakes in their quest for a cure. Even today the symbol of the medical profession and the insignia of the U.S. Army Medical Corps is a winged staff (the staff carried by Mercury as messenger of the gods) entwined by two serpents. This easily recognized symbol is known as a *caduceus*.

By the year 1553 B.C., Egyptian priests and compounders were using mixtures of crushed eggs, animal blood, turpentine, figs, animal oil, vegetables, and other animal and plant parts in the preparation of prescriptions. The famous Ebers Papyrus scroll, which dates back to 1552 B.C., contains names of drugs, formulas, and cosmetics used by Egyptians. By 600 B.C., the ancient empire of Babylonia boasted of practitioners whose wine remedies had to be taken in accord with the movements of various planetary bodies. This form of heavenly medical practice served as a forerunner to astrology, which professes to interpret the influence of planetary bodies on human affairs.

It is difficult to separate the Greek and Roman schools of medical practice because the Romans adopted many customs and traditions from the Greeks. Greek physicians competed with priests who believed that demons were responsible for illness, and temples served as centers of worship as well as therapy. The famous Greek physician Hippocrates (c. 460–360 B.C.), who became known as the Father of Medicine, introduced the scientific method to the art of healing. Hippocrates was a clinician who studied the symptoms of patients and dismissed the concept of magical or supernatural intervention in the incidence of disease. Hippocrates served as his own pharmacist and prepared inhalations, suppositories, lozenges,

and gargles. Despite the availability of many drugs, he often stressed various diets, mild emetics, and fresh air as treatment.

Claudius Galen was a great Roman physician-pharmacist (A.D. 130–200) who studied in Greece and moved to Rome where he established a large following. Galen categorized and classified drugs according to their effectiveness against specific diseases. Many drugs used and studied by Galen were plant parts and are now referred to as *galenicals*, which distinguishes the class from chemicals or minerals. Galen originated the formula for the preparation of cold cream, which is still used today as a soothing skin softener.

The Arabian period (A.D. 700–1000) served to introduce the practice of pharmacy as separate from that of medicine. Apothecaries, referred to as *sandalani*, appeared, and in them the art of pharmacy was practiced as a blend of science and superstition. Arabian pharmacists applied principles of chemistry in the preparation of drugs and masked bad-tasting mixtures with rosewater, syrup, and citrus peels. The Arabian government regulated the practice of pharmacy, and inspectors periodically visited shops. It must be emphasized that the Arabian period gave the pharmacist a definite domain in the healing arts and separated the dispensing of drugs from the jurisdiction of the physician.

Although the Arabian period introduced separate places for the practice of pharmacy, it was the edict of a German emperor that provided the first legal division of pharmacy from medicine. The exact date of this important event is unknown, but most historians agree that somewhere between A.D. 1224 and 1240, Frederick II of Sicily declared an edict that represented a "Declaration of Independence" for pharmacists. The legislation proclaimed that an educational program for pharmacists be initiated, that pharmacists be licensed for practice, that pharmacies be inspected periodically and penalties imposed for improper dispensing and illegal sale of poi-

sons, and that a system of uniform prescription fees be maintained. The first three components of the edict of Frederick II persist in the United States and most countries of the world. The last component (related to uniformity of fees) applies in limited circumstances to pharmacists who are compensated by state governments upon filling prescriptions for patients on public assistance programs.

Apothecaries first appeared in Europe during the twelfth century, and James I of Scotland established the first poison control law in 1480. By the sixteenth century, pharmacists were preparing prescriptions that included unstable drugs, and the art of compounding and storing medicines took on added importance. In 1546 the senate of the city of Nuremberg recognized the value of standardizing drugs and ordered publication of a drug description book to ensure uniformity in the filling of prescriptions. This was the first recognized formulary of pharmaceuticals, and it was to be followed by many throughout the world in an effort to safeguard public health.

The Renaissance signaled the rebirth of independent thought. The invention of moveable type in printing made it possible to quickly transmit knowledge. Swiss physician Theophrastus Bombastus von Hohenheim (1493–1541) made an indelible impression upon pharmacy by advocating that the human body be looked upon as a system of chemicals to be treated by chemical substances rather than by limited administration of traditional plant and animal drugs. This amazing scientist assumed the alias of Paracelsus and, more than anyone else, changed pharmacy from a botany-based profession to one that includes a chemical orientation toward medicines. The work of Paracelsus, who was born one year after Columbus discovered America, had as great an impact on human-

ity as the amazing discoveries of Christopher Columbus. Paracelsus sought to treat the local origin of disease within the body using specific chemicals rather than abiding by the favored concept of disease as a disequilibrium of the entire body. Though Paracelsus eliminated some false concepts of the past, he continued to maintain mystical beliefs. Nevertheless, he must be recognized as the innovative great-grandfather of medicinal chemistry.

The followers of Paracelsus introduced countless chemical remedies during the sixteenth and seventeenth centuries. Outstanding in the eighteenth century was Swedish pharmacist Carl Wilhelm Scheele, who isolated and discovered hydrogen sulfide; benzoic, hydrofluoric, and tartaric acids; potassium permanganate; and other substances used in chemistry and pharmacy. During the latter part of the eighteenth century, the Industrial Revolution began with the invention of labor-saving devices. Machines replaced hand tools. In pharmaceutical manufacturing, three significant inventions had a major impact over a fifty-year span. In 1842, Hagner of Philadelphia produced the first drug mill, and the following year Brockeden of England invented the first tablet machine. In 1886, Limousin of France introduced the use of ampoules for containment of injectable medicines. Each of these developments influenced the growth of large-scale drug manufacturing.

The nineteenth century was fertile with important events and discoveries. Drug research escalated with the discovery of the first alkaloid, morphine, in 1815 by German pharmacist Serturner. Two French pharmacists, Caventou and Pelletier, isolated other alkaloids including quinine, strychnine, veratrine, brucine, and narceine. The first attempt to form a national association of American pharmacists resulted in the organization of the American Pharmaceutical Association on October 7, 1852. Formal education for pharmacists

in America gained impetus, and by 1864, eight colleges of pharmacy offered study programs in the profession.

The twentieth century witnessed the advent of new classes of drugs such as hormones, sulfonamides, antibiotics, tranquilizers, and radiopharmaceuticals. World War I was the starting point for phenomenal growth of the pharmaceutical industry in the United States. The war interfered with shipments of drugs from Germany and forced America to independently research and synthesize its own drug products. As a result, the drug industry in the United States developed to its present position of world leadership in the manufacturing and distribution of medicinals. International drug empires are now consolidating their efforts through mergers and takeovers to form a global network of drug manufacturers that will ultimately result in discoveries of therapeutic value for all.

Never before have the tools of research quickened science and knowledge as they do today. Never before have researchers gained as much expertise and application in their quest for curing the maladies of mankind. Gene-therapy research has emerged as a promising and groundbreaking approach to the treatment of a great number of diseases and genetic disabilities in the twenty-first century.

A tidal wave of new molecular entities (NMEs) has swept around the world including new "statin" drugs that lower cholesterol, drugs that reduce frequency of epileptic seizures, and drugs that suppress the appetite of the morbidly obese.

In 2001 the Food and Drug Administration's Center for Drug Evaluation and Research (CDER) approved sixty-six new drugs and biological products. Of the new drugs, twenty-four were NMEs containing an active ingredient that had never before been approved for use in the United States. Ten of the new drugs received priority status due to their importance regarding public health. One of

these drugs, Gleevec, is a new oral treatment for chronic myeloid leukemia, a rare and life-threatening type of cancer that affects about forty thousand people in the United States.

This chapter is but a thumbnail sketch of pharmacy's history. The profession of pharmacy, as known today, has evolved from countless social, cultural, economic, legal, political, and educational influences instigated by thousands of men and women over many centuries. Men and women entering pharmacy today will discover new drugs, shape methods of practice, lobby legislation, adapt innovations, teach future students, and set the course of destiny for this dynamic profession.

2

A Dynamic Profession

Extraordinary legal, political, economic, demographic, technical, scientific, and educational innovations have combined to transform all aspects of pharmacy practice. Pharmacists engaged in every facet of the time-honored profession are determined to successfully confront the barrage of forces that hold problems and promise to those meeting the drug needs of a demanding, sophisticated, and health-conscious society.

Education in Flux

Pharmaceutical educators and administrators have had a decisive influence upon the manner in which schools of pharmacy grant degrees. In academic year 1989–90, there were 74 schools of pharmacy with 12 of them offering only six-year doctor of pharmacy degrees, 37 offering both five-year baccalaureate in pharmacy degrees and six-year doctor of pharmacy degrees, and 25 offering only five-year baccalaureate in pharmacy degrees. Ten years later

(academic year 2000–2001), there were 83 schools of pharmacy with accredited professional degree programs. Seventy-nine now offered the doctor of pharmacy degree, 60 offered both baccalaureate in pharmacy and doctor of pharmacy degrees, and 4 schools offered baccalaureates in pharmacy as the sole degree.

Organizational Name Changes

The dawn of the twenty-first century finds numerous national pharmacy associations adopting new titles to better describe and represent the fresh objectives and ambitious goals that have recently emerged. Renaming an organization entails considerable expense and inconvenience as new stationery must be printed, acronyms often change, and journals are given new titles. Overwhelming cognizance of change prompts influential and admired associations to take this important, dramatic, and costly step.

In May 1994, the Pharmaceutical Manufacturers Association (PMA) changed its name to Pharmaceutical Research and Manufacturers of America (PhRMA) "to emphasize the expanding role of research and innovation among its members." Founded in 1958, its earlier objectives sought "to maintain consistently high standards of quality and purity for pharmaceutical and biological production and to encourage research on the development of new and better medical products and the packaging and transportation of them." An intriguing final sentence in its news release announcing the name change states, "PhRMA, with its sharply defined mission and new method of operating, is ready to be a more effective player in the effort to reshape the U.S. health-care system." The PhRMA, which represents more than one hundred research-based pharmaceutical companies including more than forty of the country's leading biotechnology companies, performs a valuable service in

proclaiming the remarkable accomplishments of American pharmaceutical firms. Of 265 major global drugs developed between 1970 and 1992, almost 50 percent were of U.S. origin.

In January 1995 the American Society of Hospital Pharmacists (ASHP), founded in 1942, officially changed its name to the American Society of Health-System Pharmacists. Fortunately the acronym ASHP remained the same. According to ASHP, a goodly number of its members are changing from involvement with independent entities (hospitals) to participation in integrated health-care systems (networks of providers including hospitals, physician group practices, nursing homes, and home-care facilities) that contract to meet the drug needs of groups such as employees of a company.

In November 1996 the National Association of Retail Druggists (NARD), founded more than one hundred years ago in 1898, changed its name to the National Community Pharmacists Association (NCPA). Public perception of local pharmacists as "retailers" began to fade step-by-step as the education and subsequent responsibilities of pharmacists shifted from commercial and mercantile aspects to principles of complex patient care related to chronic disease monitoring, drug regimens, nutrition, drug interactions, geriatric pharmacology, weight control, and countless drug-related areas too numerous to elaborate upon here. The chapter on community pharmacy practice will confirm that the inclusion of the word "retail" is no longer apropos.

FDA Pace Quickens

The Food and Drug Administration (FDA) is the middleman between the drug maker and the consumer because it regulates the safety and effectiveness of medicinals. For years critics have lam-

basted the FDA as an overly cautious bureaucracy that delays approval of new therapeutic agents, thereby depriving citizens of lifesaving medicines. Discussing the birth of a new drug, the U.S. Department of Labor's "Career Guide to Industries" (Bulletin 2453) states: "The entire process, from first testing on laboratory animals to FDA approval, may take 12 years." PhRMA notes in its "1996 Industry Profile" that total development time of investigational new drugs (INDs) grew from 8.1 years in the 1970s to 14.2 years in the 1980s to 14.8 years for drugs approved from 1990 through 1994. Recently, public pressure to streamline drug approvals has resulted in the FDA's elimination of some restrictions, consolidation of multiple applications into a single form, easing of rules allowing extrapolation of adult doses for administration to children, and adoption of the Prescription Drug User Fee Act of 1992. Under the 1992 act, drug companies are paying the FDA more than $320 million over a five-year period to help the governmental agency increase its drug review staff by six hundred scientists. In addition, individual companies now pay a $208,000 user fee with each application. In December 1996, FDA Commissioner David A. Kessler ended the year and his tenure by noting that his agency, over the past twelve months, had nearly doubled the approval rate of new "breakthrough" drugs and reduced the review process time by half.

Industrial Merger Mania

A prologue to the merger mania of the nineties took place in 1989, when American drug manufacturer SmithKline Beckman melded with transatlantic suitor Beecham Group of Britain and the merger created SmithKline Beecham. Four months later, in July 1989, a

second megamerger occurred with the marriage of American companies Bristol-Myers (twelfth largest in world drug sales) and E.R. Squibb (fifteenth largest in world drug sales) forming, at that time, the second-largest drug manufacturer. The old axiom "there's safety in numbers" came to the fore as manufacturers decided that consolidation was one strategy that would succeed in the face of fierce, global competition. Other benefits of merging include synergistic research, cost savings, penetration of new markets, and incentives/means to reduce drug prices as advocated by worldwide governmental agencies.

In May 1994 the Swiss drug maker Roche Holding Ltd. acquired the U.S. pharmaceutical company Syntex Corporation, making it the world's fourth-largest company, with combined drug sales of $11.8 billion annually. In August 1994 American Home Products swallowed the American Cyanamid Company, creating a firm with annual sales of $12.6 billion, of which $9.3 billion is in drugs and other health-care products. That same month, SmithKline Beecham grew bigger when it acquired Sterling Winthrop, the over-the-counter (o-t-c) drug enterprise of Eastman Kodak, thereby doubling its o-t-c business to more than $2 billion, or 6.66 percent of the $30 billion a year spent by consumers around the world on self-medication products.

In March 1995 the two British companies Glaxo and Wellcome merged to create the world's largest drug maker (world share of 5.3 percent), with annual sales of $12.2 billion and domination in the treatment of ulcers, herpes, and AIDS. In May 1995 the German chemical and pharmaceutical giant Hoechst A.G. bought Marion Merrell Dow (Kansas City, Missouri), creating the world's second-largest drug maker, behind Britain's Glaxo Wellcome and just ahead of America's Merck & Company. In August 1995 the U.S. com-

pany Upjohn joined forces with Pharmacia A.B. of Sweden making Pharmacia & Upjohn the world's ninth-largest pharmaceutical firm, with annual sales of $7 billion.

In March 1996 two rival Swiss pharmaceutical giants, Sandoz Ltd. and Ciba-Geigy Ltd., combined to form the world's second-largest drug maker (at that time), to be known as Novartis. They hoped to reduce expenses by $1.5 billion through mid-1999 via elimination of 13,500 jobs and the closing of duplicate plant facilities. Industrial observers believe the future will continue to hold untold twists and turns in the ever-changing arena of pharmaceutical makers.

Chain Pharmacy Takeovers

"Bigger is better" is corroborated by the wave of takeover activity among chain pharmacies in the United States during the 1990s. The National Association of Chain Drug Stores (NACDS), founded in 1933, has a membership of more than 135 chains ranging in size from a small chain of 4 pharmacies (minimum number to be classified as a chain) to a huge single chain consisting of more than 3,500 pharmacies. Between 1992 and 1996 the NACDS tracked a total of 77 chain buyouts involving transfer of approximately 8,500 pharmacy chain drugstores.

This buying boom allowed acquirers to increase market share, slash expenses, bargain and negotiate better prices from third-party providers and drug suppliers, share computer systems, gain and increase prescription volume through renewals, extend geographic reach to higher growth areas, and initiate aggressive advertising campaigns. During the final three months of 1996, three of the country's biggest pharmacy chains each acquired another chain

within the top ten drug chains (by store count). Rite Aid grew by 1,000 stores when it absorbed Thrifty Payless Inc.; Revco grew by 380 stores when it bought Big B Inc.; and JCPenney/Thrift grew by 1,700 stores when it purchased Eckerd Corp. In February 1997 CVS Corporation acquired Revco, thereby adding 2,600 pharmacies to its existing 1,408 outlets and making CVS the chain with the greatest number of pharmacies in the country.

Health-Care Innovations

The health-care system in the United States remains in a state of flux as a barrage of amendments and modifications of federal and state legislations impact and transform the pharmaceutical marketplace. Throughout the nation in 1996, approximately eight hundred bills were filed in statehouses related to health-insurance regulation, and more than eighty of them were passed by state legislatures. Practicing pharmacists have weathered the onslaught of profound economic forces and managerial pressures that have changed the face of pharmacy.

The federal Medicare program, enacted in 1965 to provide health care for the elderly, and Medicaid, administered by states with costs shared by the federal government, led slowly but surely to pharmacy's alphabet soup of HMOs (health maintenance organizations), MCOs (managed-care organizations), DURs (drug utilization reviews), and PBMs (pharmacy benefit managers).

Not that long ago, in the 1950s through 1960s, consumers paid cash, referred to as "out-of-pocket" payments, to pharmacists for 100 percent of all filled prescriptions. As the 1960s drew to a close, cash payments for prescriptions grew smaller and smaller due to the growth of third-party governmental and private payment programs.

By 1970, out-of-pocket payments for prescriptions had dwindled to just over 80 percent, by 1980 to 65 percent, and in 1995, only 42 percent of the estimated $56 billion spent that year for outpatient prescription expenditures was paid out-of-pocket. In 2000 there were 78 million people enrolled in HMOs and an additional 152 million members in MCOs, and 90 percent of them had some form of prescription drug benefits involving deductibles and/or co-payments (statistics from U.S. Centers for Medicare and Medicaid Services). Rather than being a threat, HMOs and MCOs proved to be a boon to drug sales in American pharmacies.

Today's pharmacist is no longer merely the preparer and dispenser of drugs. Slowly but surely over the years, the pharmacist has grown in stature and now assumes and carries out responsibilities as a health-system provider that hitherto were foreign to the practice of pharmacy. The home health-care pharmacist is a team member who recommends therapy regimens, requests blood tests when necessary, monitors drug programs of patients, and consults with physicians regarding patient progress. The presence of a pharmacist in an emergency department is invaluable when emergencies involve overdoses, drug side effects, complex drug interactions, drug-related illness, and dosage and drug decisions. United States Public Health pharmacists work with the Indian Health Service and carry out primary care responsibilities by obtaining a patient's history and vital signs, requesting laboratory tests, performing physical diagnostic techniques, evaluating data, and determining a treatment plan. Can anyone imagine how many words of wisdom from pharmacists to patients each day may have prevented unnecessary visits to doctors' offices and gratified countless recipients with precious, professional health counseling?

A Bright Future

According to the U.S. Department of Labor, the future of pharmacy employment is bright. The total of 217,000 pharmacists employed in 2000 is expected to grow by 24 percent, or 53,000 jobs, by the year 2010. That rate of growth is faster than average, meaning that there will be comparably more new positions in pharmacy than in many other areas. The Department of Labor states confidently that "very good opportunities are expected for licensed pharmacists." The future of pharmacy holds promise for its participants in all of its areas of specialization.

3

EDUCATIONAL REQUIREMENTS

UNTIL THE EARLY part of the nineteenth century, aspiring pharmacists in the United States had to gain credentials through the apprenticeship system. An apprentice learns a trade or profession by working for a person who has mastered the field. Today some men and women enter carpentry and plumbing trades by serving apprenticeships with master carpenters and plumbers. In horse racing, a jockey who has less than a year of experience and who has won fewer than forty races is described as an apprentice. Sole dependence upon on-the-job training for pharmacists was eliminated in 1821 when the first school of pharmacy was founded in the United States.

The Growth of Pharmaceutical Education

Though formal education in pharmacy began forty-five years after the signing of the Declaration of Independence, its development

was slow, and by 1864 there were only eight American schools of pharmacy providing professional instruction. In those early days, courses were taught at night, physicians usually gave the lectures, and the apprentice system still constituted a major portion of instruction. Of course, during this period the number of drugs used was relatively small and hand processes of dosage preparation were numerous.

The twentieth century saw the founding of the Conference of Pharmaceutical Faculties, which consisted of representatives from twenty-one pharmacy schools. In 1925 the conference changed its name to the American Association of Colleges of Pharmacy, retaining its primary objective of advancing pharmaceutical education, research, and service in all accredited institutions. Today there are eighty-three schools of pharmacy located in forty-three states, Puerto Rico, and the District of Columbia.

The evolution of pharmaceutical education in the United States reflects the dramatic changes undergone by pharmacy practice during the twentieth century. A two-year course in pharmacy was initiated at the turn of that century and prevailed until 1925, when a three-year program was mandated. In 1932 a four-year course of study leading to the baccalaureate degree in pharmacy took effect. In 1960 a preprofessional concept was incorporated that extended the pharmacy curriculum to a minimum five-year study program. A preprofessional program consists of a well-defined battery of subjects taken in preparation for the study of a profession. Professional schools of law, medicine, and dentistry had earlier adapted the concept that required applicants to satisfactorily complete prerequisite collegiate studies prior to admission. Consequently, prelaw, predentistry, and premedical students began sharing some classes with prepharmacy students at liberal arts colleges.

The American Council on Pharmaceutical Education is the national agency for accreditation of professional degree programs in pharmacy. The council is an autonomous agency whose board of directors consists of ten individuals: three appointments each from the American Association of Colleges of Pharmacy (AACP), the American Pharmaceutical Association (APA), and the National Association of Boards of Pharmacy (NABP), plus a single representative from the American Council on Education (ACE). A Public Interest Panel, which consists of at least two representatives of the public, participates in the accreditation process in an advisory capacity. The ACE appointee as well as members of the Public Interest Panel are not members of the profession nor are they involved in pharmaceutical education, thereby ensuring a public perspective in policy and decision-making processes.

Battle of the Degrees

In the past, two professional curricula culminated in the awarding of pharmacy degrees. One was a five-year curriculum that led to the baccalaureate degree in pharmacy (B.S. in pharmacy) and the second was a minimum six-year curriculum that led to the doctor of pharmacy (Pharm.D.) degree. Either degree qualified the recipient for pharmacy practice once the state licensing examination had been passed. Recently the B.S. degree has been phased out, with the Pharm.D. degree being the only option for students now considering pharmacy school.

The compendium *1997–1998 Pharmacy School Admission Requirements*, published by the American Association of Colleges of Pharmacy, states: "In July 1992, a majority of the nation's schools and colleges of pharmacy voted to move toward awarding the doc-

tor of pharmacy (Pharm.D.) degree as the only professional degree in pharmacy."

Fueled by such momentum, pharmacy's pendulum of education has swung purposively toward the six-year Pharm.D. degree (doctor of pharmacy). As of 2002, according to the American Association of Colleges of Pharmacy (aacp.org), "The B.S. program will no longer be offered in the United States to any new students. The last B.S. of Pharmacy students will graduate in 2004."

High School Highlights

The high school education consists of four years of secondary school studies from the ninth to the twelfth grade. In some public and private school systems, the four-year secondary school program may be divided between junior and senior high school studies. Courses in secondary school curricula are measured in terms of *units*. A unit is defined as one year's work on a single subject. Most high school students will study English during each of the four years in high school, thereby accumulating four units in that subject.

For admission eligibility, community colleges and universities often require applicants to complete sixteen units of acceptable high school work. Students considering pharmacy as a career should not be enrolled in vocational or nonacademic programs of high schools. Enrollment in college preparatory high school curricula will satisfy admission requirements to pharmacy schools and other institutions of higher education.

English must be included during each of the four years spent in high school. The ability to read, write, and speak intelligently is increasingly vital to the practice of pharmacy. The future pharmacy

student must have a strong foundation in science and is urged to include the three basic laboratory sciences of chemistry, biology, and physics in the high school program. Completion of the three sciences over the four-year period will provide three units of credit toward collegiate admission and lay the foundation for future college-level courses in chemistry, biology, and physics. At least two courses in mathematics should be carried, and students would do well to study the highest level of math course consistent with their ability.

Completion of English, sciences, and mathematics as described will yield nine of the sixteen units needed for collegiate admission. Remaining units may be drawn from courses in social studies, foreign language, history, and electives. A course in computer literacy must be included among elective courses. Practical skills, like knowing how to type with ten fingers instead of two, are invaluable to the pharmacist, who must type various forms and labels as part of daily prescription duties.

What other elective subjects should the high school student take? Study programs in art and music instill an appreciation for the creative process, stimulate an interest in the beauty of sight and sound, and cultivate an enjoyment of aesthetics that may endure and extend throughout life. Diverse courses enrich and inform, therefore improving future personal decisions. Subjects such as social sciences, history, theology, and philosophy provide some investigation of human conduct and principles of being. As a rule, students earn better grades in courses they enjoy. A wealth of wisdom awaits the student who selects a portfolio of courses with care; hours well invested in electives are the dividends of the high school education.

Sixteen units of acceptable high school work are often required for collegiate admission, but some institutions may require as few

as fifteen units or as many as seventeen units. The graduate of a four-year secondary school should have no difficulty meeting the unit requirements. Prior to discussing application procedures, it may be helpful to outline (as culled from pharmacy school catalogs) the typical high school curriculum now recommended by the eighteen pharmacy schools that admit students directly from high school:

High School Courses

Courses	*Units*	*Courses*	*Units*
English	4	Physics	1
Mathematics	2	Social Studies	2
Biology	1	Electives	5
Chemistry	1	**Total**	**16**

Early Admission Programs

At one time, all accredited institutions of higher education required that applicants graduate from high school prior to admission. Today there are some universities and colleges that admit outstanding secondary-school students upon completion of the third year (junior year) of high school. These early admission programs recognize the advances made in secondary-school education and the increasing maturity of today's high school students. Students admitted to college on an early admission program receive their high school diplomas following successful completion of the freshman collegiate year. State departments of education will issue diplomas upon receipt of the three-year high school transcript and the one-year college record.

This accelerated approach to education saves a year's time but entails a loss of experiences that students may later regret. By eliminating the final year of secondary school, the student misses the culmination of the high school developmental process. During the senior year there are numerous activities in progress that contribute to the socialization of the individual. Seniors in high school plan class trips, athletic affairs, proms, yearbooks, prize presentations, commencement exercises, and other events that signify the end of one cycle and the beginning of another. Vivid experiences give birth to memories and provide understanding and empathy along the way.

The student who indifferently receives the high school diploma in the mailbox has been deprived of the friendships and ceremonies that celebrate a significant event. Early admission to college provides an immediate new environment, fresh friends, and eliminates one year in the trek toward a college degree, but is the sacrifice worth it? The shortcut may not always be worth the cost in personal development and satisfaction.

Standard Tests for High School Students

A number of standard tests are administered nationally to high school students each year. These include the Scholastic Aptitude Test (SAT), American College Testing Program (ACT), and Pharmacy College Admission Test (PCAT). Students are advised to take the required tests since colleges may evaluate specific test scores in conjunction with high school transcripts.

The SAT is a three-hour examination that attempts to measure verbal and quantitative skills. The verbal score gives some indication of a student's skills in reading and understanding words, while

the mathematics score measures a student's knowledge of numbers and quantitative reasoning. The highest score possible in each area is 800 and the lowest 200. A score of 550 on each section of the test is considered average, with a combined score of approximately 1,050 accepted as median.

The ACT consists of four tests titled "English Usage," "Mathematics Usage," "Social Studies Reading," and "Natural Sciences Reading." The test also includes a student profile section that allows students to express their aspirations, needs, talents, and backgrounds. Scores are reported for each subtest in addition to a composite score. Composite scores for the ACT may range from 1 to 36 with the majority falling between 15 and 25.

The final test to confront pharmacy school applicants is the Pharmacy College Admission Test (PCAT), which is prepared and administered by The Psychological Corporation. The test, administered three times each year at testing centers, is designed to measure general academic ability and scientific aptitude. At this time, the test is required or recommended by 50 percent of the eighty-three schools of pharmacy in the United States.

This versatile test is administered at different levels to liberal arts college students as well as to high school students. Reports issued to admission offices present applicants' scores in the areas of verbal ability, quantitative ability, biology, chemistry, and reading comprehension, with "norms" that permit pharmacy colleges to compare applicants with students entering comparable curriculum patterns. Students pay an examination fee of $69 to The Psychological Corporation that also includes the mailing of scores to applicants and three pharmacy schools. Applicants may have scores mailed to more than three pharmacy schools by paying $16 for each school beyond the three-school limit. An annual brochure, the *PCAT Announcement Booklet*, which includes testing center information, dates of

examinations, an application form, and sample questions, is available free of charge by contacting:

The Psychological Corporation
555 Academic Court
San Antonio, Texas 78204
(800) 622-3231
Fax: (210) 339-8711
tpcweb.com/pse/pcat

Prepharmacy College Requirements

The moment a student chooses pharmacy as a vocation is the moment when communication must be initially established with one or more schools of pharmacy. By requesting a free catalog or bulletin from a school of pharmacy, a student learns of the requirements that must be met prior to admission, as well as much additional pertinent information (for example, curriculum, tuition, admission requirements, financial assistance, dormitory accommodations, crime on campus, student services, academic calendar, grading system, faculty-student ratio, extracurricular activities, and physical facilities). Students may also obtain information by browsing college home pages on the Internet.

All of the eighty-three schools of pharmacy (see Appendix C for a complete list) in the United States fall into one of two institutional categories. A pharmacy school is either a stand-alone institution or one that is affiliated with a university. The stand-alone college is defined as a private, independent institution of higher learning within which a student is able to complete prepharmacy and pharmacy courses. The pharmacy school affiliated with a university will usually encourage applicants to satisfy prepharmacy

requirements at the university's liberal arts college prior to transfer to the pharmacy school.

University-affiliated pharmacy schools will also admit students who complete preprofessional courses at other accredited liberal arts, community, or junior colleges; as will stand-alone private, independent pharmacy schools. For students pursuing baccalaureate in pharmacy degrees, the final three years of professional study of the total five-year program must be completed in a pharmacy school (2–3 program). For students pursuing doctor of pharmacy degrees, the final four years of the total six-year program must be completed in a pharmacy school (2–4 program).

The prepharmacy courses outlined below represent the preprofessional courses required for admission by a majority of pharmacy schools in the United States for entrance into baccalaureate in pharmacy degree or doctor of pharmacy degree programs.

First-Year Prepharmacy Courses

Courses	Semester Hours
English/Public Speaking	6
General Chemistry [a]	8
General Biology (Botany and Zoology) [a]	8
Mathematics [b]	6
Electives [c]	2–4
Total	30–32

---

a Must include a laboratory component.

b Some schools require calculus-level mathematics.

c Recommended electives include sociology, psychology, and other behavioral sciences.

Second-Year Prepharmacy Courses

Courses	Semester Hours
Organic Chemistry [a]	8
Physics [a]	8
Introductory Economics	2–4
Electives [c]	10–12
Total	30–32

Exceptions and Variations

A semester hour is the unit devised to measure college credits. The semester hour credit for a lecture course is equal to the number of hours spent in the classroom per week. The student who carries three hours of English per week for one semester (usually sixteen weeks) has completed three semester hours of credit if the course is satisfactorily passed at the end of the semester. A single laboratory session (consisting of three to four consecutive hours) per week is usually evaluated as one semester hour of credit. A chemistry course with three hours of lecture and one laboratory session per week would carry a credit of four semester hours. A college student normally carries sixteen hours per semester, and since there are two semesters in the academic year, a total of thirty to thirty-two semester hours should be completed per academic year. The usual two-year prepharmacy requirement is sixty semester hours of designated course work.

There are, of course, variations from one school to another, and students are reminded to communicate with the school of their

---

a Must include a laboratory component.

c Recommended electives include sociology, psychology, and other behavioral sciences.

choice to be certain of specific admission requirements. A school of pharmacy may include microbiology or anatomy as part of the preprofessional program, although most pharmacy schools now include these courses of instruction at the professional program level. It is also recognized that semester-hour credit for courses like organic chemistry, physics, and biology may vary from one community college to another. However, schools of pharmacy recognize these differences and are flexible in their semester-hour requirements for specific courses. For example, in some liberal arts institutions, the course in general chemistry may carry as few as six semester hours of credit and the course in organic chemistry as many as twelve semester hours. Most important to the student is a solid foundation of basic knowledge in the sciences of chemistry, biology, and physics.

A major advantage of the 2–3 baccalaureate in pharmacy program and the 2–4 Pharm.D. program is that they permit applicants to complete two years of prepharmacy study at any accredited institution. All of the courses in the preprofessional program are readily available in community colleges or universities, so students have the option of selecting colleges that are most convenient for them. Community colleges have gained support in many states that use public funds to provide low-cost higher education programs for their residents.

The student who selects a college close to home enjoys immediate economic advantage because of possible lower tuition, no dormitory room and board fees, and availability of public transportation. The student who continues to live at home for this two-year span also avoids countless other incidental costs that can add up over the two-year prepharmacy period. Continuing to live at home reduces laundry costs, lessens entertainment expenses, may allow students to keep part-time jobs, and encourages them to save

for future away-from-home college expenses. The college student at home avoids the cost of traveling great distances from college to enjoy weekends or holidays with friends and relatives.

The student in a preprofessional program at a liberal arts college has the opportunity to communicate with students majoring in many disciplines. In the typical liberal arts college, a chemistry class will include people majoring in premed, predentistry, engineering, education, and countless other fields, thereby affording the prepharmacy student the chance to meet students with varied interests and motivations. Sometimes these encounters help confirm career decisions and goals.

Pharm.D.1 and Pharm.D.2 Degrees

Pharmaceutical educators have adopted a jargon that differentiates doctor of pharmacy degrees according to the manner in which they were earned. Pharm.D. degrees earned as first and only professional degrees, via completion of "straight thru" curricula of two years of prepharmacy and four years of professional courses, are referred to as Pharm.D.1 degrees. Pharm.D. degrees earned as postbaccalaureate degrees, via completion of additional study as prescribed by a pharmacy school, are referred to as Pharm.D.2 degrees.

Putting it simply, a baccalaureate in pharmacy graduate is able to earn a Pharm.D.2 degree by gaining admission to a pharmacy school and following a study program as prescribed by the faculty of the institution. Only the timing and manner of study distinguishes Pharm.D.1 from Pharm.D.2 degrees.

In 2000–2001, according to the American Association of Colleges of Pharmacy, schools of pharmacy collectively granted Pharm.D.2 degrees to 979 pharmacists who had previously earned baccalaureate in pharmacy degrees. The fact that increasing num-

bers of baccalaureates in pharmacy are willing to return to school, for anywhere from one to three years dependent upon the school's policy and whether the returning student is full-time or part-time, confirms the popularity, acceptance, and importance of the doctor of pharmacy degree. For a complete list of pharmacy schools and degrees offered (B.S. in pharmacy, Pharm.D.1, and Pharm.D.2), see Appendix C.

4

Pharmacy School Admissions

There are several important steps to take as you go through the process of applying to pharmacy school, and it all begins with an application form. If you are accepted at your school of choice, you will have to think about how to finance your education. Some options are offered here. If you are not accepted, the suggestions outlined later in this chapter will show you how you might change that outcome on your next try.

The Application Process

The individual who displays "application etiquette" will benefit immeasurably; observing the conventional requirements during the application procedure always facilitates response. An important element of application etiquette is transmitting complete, precise, and relevant information to the admissions officer, beginning with the first inquiry.

Obtaining an Application

Much of the information you'll need to apply to a pharmacy program can be found online at the school's website. Some schools will have you fill out an online form to request an application, while some schools' applications can be downloaded and printed. Other schools prefer that you complete and submit your application electronically. Find out what options are available at the schools you're interested in, and try to use the school's preferred method of application submission. Whether you're using a paper or electronic application form, be sure to read all the instructions before you complete and submit it.

The Application Fee

Most applications require submission of an application fee, so be sure to include a check or money order in the right amount made payable to the institution in question. The applicant who returns the application without the fee has created a situation that involves needless correspondence and paperwork. Many a comedy of errors has resulted when applicants remember application fees the day after the forms have been mailed to colleges. The applicant hurriedly mails the check to the college, but by that time the college has returned the incomplete application to the applicant. Some colleges hold the application and will not act on it until the check is in receipt. A bigger, but still common, problem exists when colleges receive checks for which there are insufficient funds in applicants' checking accounts. It sometimes takes months for a check to be returned by the bank to the college bursar, who then notifies the admissions office of the deficiency. The admissions officer must then communicate with the applicant about the bad check, and the

applicant is frequently charged a penalty fee, in addition to the application fee, to compensate for the extra paperwork and personnel involved. Be sure to conduct your first collegiate financial transaction with finesse! Simply follow these directions:

1. Make the check payable to the institution (not to the admissions officer).
2. Make certain the amount of the check equals the application fee.
3. Be sure you mail the check and the application in the same envelope.
4. Make certain your checking account has sufficient funds to cover the check.

Credentials and Recommendation Letters

You should have an application on file in the admissions office before any additional credentials are forwarded in support of the application. Upon receipt of a student's application, the admissions office automatically creates an applicant's folder into which all related materials are filed. It is important to provide credentials to admissions offices in chronological order. When a student's transcript arrives before the application, the admissions officer is uncertain whether the transcript has arrived at the right place. Read the application and/or catalog instructions carefully and forward only what is required. Depending on the school in question, applicants may have to forward high school records, college transcripts, test scores, and recommendation letters. Some 2–3 schools require only college transcripts, so why contact your high school and ask someone to mail your high school record only to have the college admissions office receive and discard it?

In addition to transcripts, many schools require recommendation letters from your teachers or professors. It's best to ask for recommendations from teachers who are familiar with your work and in whose classes you did well. On the other hand, you may have a special relationship with a teacher in whose class you didn't get top grades. Talk to that teacher and ask if he or she would be willing to write a recommendation highlighting other important qualities such as your hard work and determination in the face of difficult subject matter. Whomever you ask, make sure that you allow ample time for your teacher to write the letter, as he or she may be writing letters for many of your other classmates, too. Also be sure to provide your teacher, if necessary, with stamped, addressed envelopes to send the letter to your schools of choice. If you're asking for a recommendation from a teacher whose class you were in a few years ago, it may be a good idea to provide him or her with a few samples of your best work from that class. This will help refresh the teacher's memory of your particular strengths.

Do provide the school's complete mailing address for those who will be sending transcripts, test scores, and letters on your behalf. Some universities have schools of medicine, dentistry, pharmacy, business, education, art, and music; often each school within the university has a separate admissions office. The responsible applicant will make a concerted effort to guarantee that all mailings related to admission are directed to the proper office within the institution.

The Interview

Once the admissions officer has received all credentials, the applicant may be invited for an interview. The interview process serves primarily as a medium of direct communication between the appli-

cant and the school rather than as a tool of evaluation. The interview provides the applicant an opportunity to visit the school and ask questions directly. Most interviews are conducted on campus, but some schools do arrange interviews at the geographical convenience of the applicant (sometimes conducted by alumni volunteers). Not all schools of pharmacy require interviews. Even if an interview is not required, applicants should make it a point to personally visit a school before making a commitment to attend. Some vacationers investigate travel accommodations more thoroughly than students examine the schools where they will spend the next three to six years.

Evaluation tools available to an admissions officer include transcripts, test scores, letters of recommendation, and interview encounters. Unquestionably the transcript is the most important and reliable tool of all. To an admissions officer, the transcript is the student's academic fingerprint. It represents grades earned by one student over a period of time from dozens of instructors teaching as many courses. Some admissions officers may consider one-shot test scores as supplementary tools of evaluation. Applicants solicit letters of recommendation from persons who will write favorably on their behalf, and, as a result, such letters have little significance in the admissions procedure unless extenuating circumstances, such as illness or special problems, are involved. The interview, though considered an evaluation tool by some, is really a direct, mutual source of information helpful to the admissions procedure.

Tuition and Financial Aid

The educational cost of becoming a pharmacist is greatly influenced by the planning of students and their parents. Those who plan in

advance may be able to considerably reduce the costs, which appear to be spiraling upward with each passing year. Proper planning involves studying the bulletins of several schools; comparing tuitions, dormitory fees, and commuting fees; and filing appropriate financial aid forms in concert with applications to schools.

However, lack of money should never prevent an academically qualified student from becoming a pharmacist. Getting through college may require working at odd jobs, borrowing funds, seeking scholarships, attending interviews with financial aid personnel, visiting banks, and showing lots of perseverance; but pursuing the career of a lifetime easily compensates for the extra effort. Each year more than $50 billion are available in grants, scholarships, low-interest loans, and work-study funds to men and women seeking financial assistance for higher education. Prepharmacy and pharmacy students with need are eligible for substantial sums of this vast pool of financial assistance, and many dedicated experts work full-time to accommodate them.

The General Accounting Office reported in 1996 that tuitions at public colleges increased 234 percent between the 1980–81 and 1994–95 school years. Tuition for in-state students at public colleges for the 1995–96 school year ranged from $1,524 to $5,521, whereas the average tuition at a four-year private college was $18,000 annually. By 2001, tuition for in-state students at a four-year public college had increased to $3,506 a year (combined tuition/room and board was approximately $8,655). Private college tuition was $15,531 a year (combined tuition/room and board was approximately $21,907). (Source: National Center for Education Statistics, *Digest of Education Statistics*, 2001.)

The average first-year tuition and fees for the Pharm.D. program in 2002–03 was $10,946 for the in-state student and $17,109 for the out-of-state student. These averages do not reflect the fact

that the annual tuition at schools of pharmacy may range from as low as $2,300 to a high of $28,000!

Those requiring financial assistance should seek advice upon entering their senior year of high school. Guidance may come from high school counselors, but students should also consult college bulletins and write to financial officers in colleges. The available aid is so diverse that it is impossible for any one counselor to be aware of all sources of assistance. Counselors may help, but it is up to the student to search out every possible source of funding.

Often the most obvious contacts for financial assistance are overlooked. The student interested in pharmacy would be wise to speak with community pharmacists and obtain the names and addresses of county and state pharmacy associations. County pharmacy associations often sponsor scholarships that are limited to locals. Chain pharmacies are another source of loan and scholarship funds; such loans can establish lifetime ties between future employers and employees. Local clubs, lodges, fraternal orders, chambers of commerce, religious organizations, and ethnic societies provide grants and scholarships to students, and individuals are urged to consult appropriate groups within the community. Parents may help by consulting their employers, as some companies provide educational benefits to children of employees. Legislators of local and state governments should be contacted to investigate the availability of funds in particular communities. Most significant is the element of timing when applying to city, state, and federal agencies offering assistance to college students.

Federal student aid programs for prepharmacy undergraduate students include Pell Grants, Supplemental Educational Opportunity Grants, college work-study, Perkins Loans, and Guaranteed Student Loans. These grants and loans are usually available at relatively low interest rates to part-time and full-time students. Need

and expenses of education determine the loan amounts. The maximum award is different for each program and depends upon various factors, such as whether the student is dependent or independent. Repayment on loans begins within specified times following degree completion. Applications are available from banks, financial aid offices, and regional offices of the United States Department of Education. In 1980 the federal government introduced a source of funds for educational purposes called Parent Loans for Undergraduate Students (PLUS). These PLUS funds are available to parents of matriculating students from any local bank and provide parents with loans capped at 9 percent. Interest is adjusted annually by the Department of Education. The interest rate was 4.86 percent for the 2002–03 school year. The funds may be borrowed for a period of ten years. For additional information or questions, contact this source at parentplusloan.com.

Health Education Assistance Loans (HEAL) originate from a federal program for fourth- and fifth-year baccalaureate in pharmacy students and fourth-, fifth-, and sixth-year doctor of pharmacy students who demonstrate need. Under the HEAL program, pharmacy students may borrow up to $12,500 per academic year to a maximum of $50,000. Pharmacy Health Profession Loans are available to students enrolled in the professional curriculum of a school of pharmacy. Pharmacy students may borrow a maximum of $2,500 plus the cost of tuition under this program. Repayment of Pharmacy Health Profession Loans must be made within a ten-year period following the separation of a student from a school of pharmacy.

Scholarships in Cyberspace

For additional scholarship sleuthing, computer-savvy students can also consult the first free online scholarship-tracking service. Fast-

WEB, available to students and parents since August 1995, has a database of more than eight hundred thousand scholarships totaling in excess of $1 billion and is a significant player in the multimillion-dollar scholarship-search industry. The Web address for this cyberspace search, where students do their own data entries, is fast web.com.

Financial aid officers in schools of pharmacy evaluate the needs of individual students and utilize work-study funds whereby jobs are provided in campus libraries, dormitories, laboratories, offices, and cafeterias. The amount of time a student may work is determined by need, class schedule, academic progress, and health status. There are many ways to meet the costs of higher education and many experts willing to help you along the way.

Student Debt

In 1984 students and parents collectively borrowed $7.9 billion to meet expenses for higher education. At the close of 1994, just ten years later, the amount had grown to $23.1 billion, according to Department of Education figures. Total borrowing had increased to $33.1 billion in the year 2000. The combined number of loans increased from 6,483,000 in 1994 to 8,618,000 in 2000 (data from *The Budget of the U.S. Government Appendix, Fiscal Years 1996– 2002*). Student debt has grown because of rising costs of tuition, higher loan limits, expanded eligibility, and greater proportion of aid in loan forms rather than grant awards and scholarships.

In 2000 the Department of Health and Human Services announced that 1.674 million health professionals had defaulted on student loans totaling $169 million under the Health Education Assistance Loan program. The majority of defaulters under this program were chiropractors (52 percent), allopathic physicians (12

percent), and dentists (19 percent). In January 1997 the Department of Education announced that, of overall students who should have begun repaying federal general student loans in 1994, 10.7 percent were in default, down from the peak of 22.4 percent in 1992, when student defaults cost taxpayers $1.7 billion. To overcome this problem, the government is getting tough on student-loan defaulters by first withholding their tax refunds and then garnishing their wages. In addition, hundreds of schools with high default rates are being dropped from federal loan programs.

The urgent need for students to borrow tuition funds and other costs of higher education cannot be denied, but students must observe discretion when it comes to the imprudent use of credit cards for other purposes. Issuers of credit cards aggressively market their services to young and inexperienced college students. According to the U.S. Department of Education, National Center for Education Statistics, *1999–2000 National Postsecondary Student Aid Study*, 47.95 percent of college students had one credit card and 28.5 percent of students had two or more credit cards. The average balance due on all credit cards was $2,864. Indiscriminate use of credit cards that charge outrageous rates of interest is responsible for plunging many a student into deep debt. Colleges and universities should think twice before endorsing or sponsoring credit cards for their students who interpret academic sanction as a reason to charge to excess.

Admission to a School of Pharmacy

The academically qualified student who applies to schools of pharmacy within specified time frames will usually be accepted. It is true that all schools of pharmacy have enrollment limits, and some

offer priority to residents of the states in which they are located. However, schools do not consider race, religion, marital status, sex, or age in the selection of applicants. Federal legislation forbids inclusion of questions related to these characteristics on application forms. A question related to disability may appear on applications, but schools need this information to provide services to students with special needs. Keep in mind that community pharmacists, hospital pharmacists, pharmacy professors, and pharmacy deans were once anxious applicants going through the same procedures of filing applications, submitting credentials, and waiting for responses from admissions officers.

Qualified applicants who apply in time, submit credentials properly, and promptly forward tuition deposits on notification of admission will soon find themselves on the way to completing an education in pharmacy. Rejected applicants to schools of pharmacy who really want to be pharmacists will not easily abandon hope. The applicant who listlessly accepts defeat and abruptly turns to another objective is probably better off for the decision. The rejected applicant with strong motivation will seek counseling and try again. There are no instant solutions, but patience, fortitude, perseverance, and cooperation will help restore the rejected applicant.

The Rejected Applicant

The rejected pharmacy applicant is one who has been denied admission to the school of choice and to other institutions offering the pharmacy degree. The applicant should attempt to gain admission to at least five schools of pharmacy before accepting the fact that qualifications for admission are lacking. Rejection letters from admissions officers do not always elaborate upon reasons for refusal

of admission. Most rejections consist of a brief but polite statement that admission has been denied.

The rejected applicant must take time to evaluate the circumstances that led to what appears to be a dead end. Introspection begins with scrutinizing one's credentials and honest self-evaluation. Schools of pharmacy do not reject applicants because of their race, religion, ethnicity, gender, economic status, age, or physical disability. The honest candidate must conclude that deficient academic credentials are responsible for denial of admission.

The applicant to a school of pharmacy is in competition with many other men and women for a limited number of places in an entering class. It is reasonable to assume that unknown rivals have won places because of superior grades in course work required for admission.

The new high school graduate who has been denied admission has a simple course of action and need not suffer any serious setback. This situation calls for admission to any community college, junior college, or liberal arts institution. During two years of study, the student will have the opportunity to satisfactorily complete college-level courses and then reapply to the school of pharmacy for admission.

The rejected applicant may have to repeat some subjects that were not satisfactorily completed the first time around in a liberal arts institution. Most colleges use a grading system of letters as follows:

A = excellent
B = good
C = fair
D = passing
F = failure

Courses passed with a grade of D do not carry transfer credit to another institution, so the rejected applicant must repeat all courses completed with grades of D. It is to the applicant's advantage to gain a solid foundation in basic science courses such as general chemistry, biology, and mathematics. Upon repeating these courses, the student must not be satisfied with grades of C. Since subject matter is being studied for the second time, this advantage should result in grades of A or B. Failure to earn A or B grades in courses of general chemistry, biology, or mathematics the second time they are taken may be an indication that the rejected applicant should pursue another objective. If a candidate for admission is rejected because of failure in a single course, the applicant may be able to repeat the course in a summer session and then take a second year of liberal arts courses required for admission. The determined applicant will consult with admissions officers of pharmacy schools for guidance and counseling. Pharmacy admissions officers are anxious to help the rejected applicant, but the applicant must demonstrate his or her enthusiasm for striving toward the goal of admission.

Courses completed with mediocre grades during the two-year preprofessional period should be repeated, but it may also be possible for students to demonstrate their ability by completing limited advanced courses. Some courses taught in pharmacy schools during the upper years, such as microbiology, physiology, biochemistry, and anatomy, may be taken at liberal arts colleges by students wishing to prove themselves. An advantage of this plan of study is that applicants may be granted advance credit for these courses upon admission to a school of pharmacy. Rejected applicants are again reminded that it is best to seek guidance and counseling from pharmacy admissions officers before undertaking any plan of study.

Guidelines for Success

The student embarking on a career in pharmacy begins an exciting voyage that will occupy more than six thousand hours of time in lectures and laboratories. The greatest challenge to a college student involves self-discipline in the skillful budgeting of free time. The successful student will appropriate free time wisely and, from the very beginning, make a firm commitment to maintain a sensible balance among hours devoted to study, diversion, and employment. The temptation to attend every party, dance, or social and sporting event must be held in check, as must the desire to maintain excessive gainful employment.

Students who flounder in college usually do so because of failure to appropriate time properly when not in scheduled lecture and laboratory meetings. Financial necessity may require a student to work at a job, but too often this work is undertaken at the expense of academic progress. The student who ignores academic assignments because of employment is as guilty as the student who spends excessive time pursuing social diversions. The earnings from employment will hardly compensate for a year's loss if the student fails and must then repeat a year with extra costs. A year's delay in graduation means that a pharmacist's income has been postponed for one year, and there is no gain in this chain of events. The professional student must allocate time with one objective in mind: the academic accountability of studenthood! Following graduation will be a lifetime of employment and diversion.

Ten College Commandments

1. **Do not cut class.** Absence from scheduled lectures and laboratories is inexcusable. Regular attendance is a must. Students who

cut are cheating themselves of the education that has been paid for in full.

2. **Do not neglect your health.** Whether the student lives at home or in a dormitory, every effort must be made to preserve health through diet and rest. Eating balanced meals, exercising daily, and getting sufficient rest prepare the student physically and mentally for a vigorous program of study.

3. **Do not copy another student's work.** The student who copies another student's work has much more to lose than the fullest understanding of the project in question. Professors are quick to recognize plagiarism and justifiably regard it as dishonest.

4. **Do not accept the words of upper-class students as sacred.** Every student should be skeptical when it comes to accepting advice from upper-class students. Well-meaning seasoned students sometimes provide inaccurate or biased personal impressions of teachers and courses to new students. Accept each course and instructor as equally important to your development as a pharmacist.

5. **Do not purchase or sell used textbooks.** Most courses in the pharmacy curriculum are taught with the use of standard texts designated by instructors. The student should buy new books that are free of the underlining and notations of previous owners. Students who buy used books from other students may unknowingly receive old editions that are lacking current information.

When a course has been completed, its assigned text should not be sold. Pharmacy courses build upon one another, and the old text may serve as a helpful reference for future subjects. By keeping all books, the student builds a library that is helpful during student years and will assist the pharmacy graduate in everyday practice.

6. **Do not delay in transcribing lecture notes.** Notes taken in lectures are written rapidly and often in abbreviated form. The note taker of dictated material must write quickly to keep pace with the

lecturer. Sometimes students invent their own shorthand symbols that designate words or phrases. It is to the student's advantage to rewrite lecture notes the same day that the original material was copied in class. Rewritten lecture notes for each course should be kept in separate spiral notebooks so they are permanently bound in chronological order. Copying lecture notes serves as a review of the professor's lecture and provides easy-to-read notes for future study at examination time. Do not lend this carefully compiled spiral notebook to fellow students. An apology for a misplaced notebook cannot compensate for the loss of hours of note transcription. If a friend wishes to compare notes, insist that it be done in your home. Do not take the finished spiral notebook to class with you; it is irreplaceable. Keep it at home where it is always available for study.

7. **Do not neglect homework.** Homework is a task assigned by the professor for the student's benefit. The student who tackles the homework assignment with that understanding gains from the experience. Homework is usually due on a specific date, and deadlines must be met. Allow sufficient time to complete homework, and avoid losing points because of late submission. Late homework stands on its own and may earn a demerit because of inconvenience to the instructor and delinquency on the part of the student.

8. **Do not study with irregularity.** As each semester's schedule is obtained, the student should allocate study hours for specific subjects on each evening and weekend. Once lecture notes are transcribed, it is a good idea to study not only recent entries but also the complete spiral notebook. Allow for relaxation between study hours. During relaxation periods a student may listen to music, visit or phone a friend, take a walk, or nap. Most important is to stick with a schedule. Once the schedule is established, it will be easier to maintain.

9. **Do not cram.** Students who cram are those who study for an examination by hastily memorizing facts at the last minute. They may be able to memorize some facts but will be unable to understand and assimilate the course content. Cramming signals failure to study with regularity during the entire semester. The student who crams has indulged in activities unrelated to the problem at hand and must now make up for negligence and procrastination. Cramming involves late hours and lack of sleep.

There is no excuse for the need to cram. The student who begins to prepare for final examinations from the first week of the semester will put in an average evening of study the night before a final, get a good evening's sleep, and take the examination with confidence and calmness.

10. **Do not resort to drugs.** Students who introduce drugs into the body's natural dynamics interfere with its balance of forces. The use of stimulants to study long into the night will result in damage and poor body control the following day. The use of depressants to fall asleep is dangerously habit-forming. Drugs are not accessories of education and serve no use on the college campus. The curriculum of the pharmacy school imparts the wisdom of drug avoidance to its students. The pharmacist knows that drugs are best used to combat disease and alleviate pain. Should a classmate offer an upper or a downer as a study aid, it is best to decline. Do not desecrate your body with drugs. Respect it. It's the only one you have.

5

PROFESSIONAL STUDY: THE PHARMACY SCHOOL CURRICULUM

ACCORDING TO THE American Association of Colleges of Pharmacy, the five specific goals of a professional pharmacy degree program are designed to produce pharmacists who will:

1. Provide pharmaceutical care to patients
2. Develop and manage medication distribution and control systems
3. Manage the pharmacy
4. Promote public health
5. Provide drug information and education

The curricula of all pharmacy schools are designed to yield the education and training necessary for graduates to gain professional competence as practitioners of pharmacy. The dynamics of phar-

maceutical education reflect the astonishing changes undergone by pharmacy practice in the United States during the twentieth century. Schools of pharmacy at the turn of that century stressed elegance in the hand preparation of pharmaceuticals; then in the thirties attention shifted to commercial aspects and business management. An emphasis on pharmaceutical chemistry evolved in the forties, and pharmacology (dealing with the effects of drugs on body organs) gained importance as a subject in the fifties.

The sixties witnessed adoption of physical pharmacy and biopharmaceutics as part of the curriculum. Subjects related to clinical pharmacy and patient relations dominated the seventies and eighties. Instruction in the nineties included the ramifications of an electronic pharmacy as simple working computers and copy machines were abetted by fax machines, electronic online billing for third-party prescription claims, modems and phone lines, bar coding for point-of-sale (POS) systems, database touch screens that generate medication information leaflets for patients, and computerized drug dispensing systems.

The current role of the pharmacist is increasingly one of human service. All trends in the practice of pharmacy point to expanding human involvement. Economic, cultural, medical, social, and psychological forces within society demand increased patient relations for the pharmacist.

Prompted by an awareness of the intricate social complex in which health professionals are gaining involvement, educators in pharmacy, medical, and nursing schools have recognized the exigency of including behavioral sciences in curricula. Changes in this direction were slow in coming because of increasing demands on the attention of the pharmacist by vast technologic knowledge advanced through drug research.

Curriculum Content

The pharmacist may be unequivocally described as the specialist whose expertise in drug therapy is unmatched by any other member of the health-care delivery team. The pharmacist serves physicians, nurses, dentists, other health practitioners, and the public at large by providing information on selection, use, formulation, storage, and administration of medicinal agents. The professional years of study in a school of pharmacy, built upon the preprofessional foundation, provide students with sufficient experience, knowledge, and skills to enter a challenging arena of health-care delivery in which learning and scholarship never cease. Course titles, contents, and sequences may vary from one school to another, but all curricula include courses that may be grouped under several principal areas of study.

Social and Administrative Sciences

Practicing pharmacists must deal with the management requirements of their responsibilities. Pharmacy administration courses prepare the student by providing information about legal, business, economic, managerial, and social/behavioral aspects of pharmacy practice. Law courses focus upon state and federal legislation related to pharmacy practice and enable the student to recognize and understand fundamental legal concepts that regulate drug distribution. Pharmaceutical economics courses deal with private and government health insurance plans, marketing principles, records and control systems, financial management, personnel relations, computer applications, and pharmacy operations. Social and behavioral components of instruction, recently added to the discipline of pharmacy administration, deal with professional communication

expected from pharmacists by patients with health problems. Introductory economics and basic social sciences studied during the prepharmacy program provide the foundation for these professional pharmacy administration courses.

Pharmaceutical Chemistry

Completion of general chemistry and organic chemistry in the preprofessional segment prepares the student for advanced chemistry courses in the pharmacy curriculum. Biochemistry, medicinal chemistry, and pharmaceutical chemistry courses are essential components of the professional curriculum. Biochemistry deals with the chemistry of living matter, enzymes and drug metabolism, and diseases caused by malfunctions of metabolic activities and biochemical systems. Medicinal chemistry is concerned with relationships of chemical structures of drugs to their biological activities in the body. The medicinal chemist synthesizes drugs with the knowledge that specific chemical structures will produce anticipated actions in the body. Students are taught to relate drug structure to drug action and to understand molecular mechanisms of drug action. Pharmaceutical chemistry courses may include toxicology (concerned with poisonous materials in biologic systems), radiopharmaceuticals (the application of radioactive drugs for diagnosis and therapy in nuclear medicine), and environmental science (disease entities due to environmental pollutants).

Pharmaceutics and Biopharmaceutics

Pharmaceutics and biopharmaceutics are sciences concerned with physical-chemical properties of drugs and the significance of these properties to the drug's absorption, distribution, metabolism, and excretion within and from the body. A drug's dosage form (capsule,

tablet, injection, ointment, lotion, aerosol, suspension, and so forth) helps determine the speed of action, intensity, duration, and effect of a drug. Introductory physics and mathematics are necessary prepharmacy courses that act as vital stepping-stones to an understanding of advanced physical science courses such as principles of pharmacokinetics and bioavailability.

Pharmacology

Pharmacology is a medical science dealing with drug action on living systems and their constituent parts. Courses that originate from pharmacology include pharmacodynamics, pharmacotherapy, and therapeutics. Pharmacodynamics is concerned with responses of normal, healthy living organisms to chemical influence and drug action. Pharmacotherapy, on the other hand, deals with organisms in a pathologic state and their responses to chemical stimuli. Therapeutics is an advanced pharmacology course with disease orientation that emphasizes clinical aspects and mechanisms of drug action. Early in the professional program, prior to studying pharmacology, students master anatomy and physiology, which are basic sciences dealing respectively with animal structure and functions of body organs. A logical program prepares the student for forthcoming courses in anatomy, physiology, and pharmacology through completion of basic biology in the prepharmacy program.

Clinical Pharmacy Clerkships

The final sequence of study in the pharmacy curriculum is the clinical clerkship. Clinical aspects are those concerned with actual observation and treatment of disease in patients rather than artificial experimentation or simulation of reality. Clinical pharmacy embraces patient orientation for the student through observation

and communication with patients in community and institutional pharmacy settings. Pharmacy practice has always been clinical because the pharmacist is the member of the health-care delivery team who communicates with the greatest number of people in any single day. The pharmacist of yesteryear regularly provided clinical services to patients seeking drug advice on injuries, burns, colds, and miscellaneous medical problems and who were too poor to seek the counsel of a physician. From 1920 to 1950, pharmacists had less available knowledge of therapeutics, as did all health professionals, but they had more time to communicate directly with visitors to the pharmacy than they do today.

Recent social, legislative, economic, and medical forces stimulated radical changes in drug dispensing and health-care delivery, which produced better-informed pharmacists and physicians but, along the way, alienated practitioners from patients. Physicians discontinued house calls and remained in their offices while pharmacists retreated to their busy prescription laboratories, minimizing patient contact. Clinical pharmacy courses in drug information, disease states, patient records, behavioral aspects of illness, and chart review are designed to restore patient relationships enjoyed by pharmacists in the past and to rekindle the humanistic spark that provides full benefit of medical progress to patients. Pharmacy schools now supervise clinical clerkships that rotate students among hospital emergency departments, community pharmacies, hospital wards and pharmacies, health centers, ambulatory-care clinics, long-term care centers, nursing homes, and even industrial settings.

Schools of pharmacy continue to fine-tune the content of the clinical year that crowns the six-year-long doctor of pharmacy (Pharm.D.) program. This final year of study has developed into a forty-week clerkship that sends students into environments they've not entered previously, such as hospital emergency rooms,

patients' bedsides, geriatric homes, psychiatric wards, home-care settings, health maintenance centers, acute-care facilities, hospital staff seminars, nutrition conferences, and countless other experiential surroundings. Seniors may even travel across state borders to satisfy these requirements. Direct, face-to-face communication with physicians, pharmacists, nurses, and other health service professionals in actual practice settings during balanced rotations serve to endow future pharmacists with the necessary experience and knowledge to partner the provision of impeccable health care to the community.

The New Internship

The innovative clerkships of pharmacy schools have supplanted in part or in whole the monitored "intern/preceptor" program, whereby pharmacy students worked weekends, evenings, and summers in local pharmacies for a set number of hours. The National Association of Boards of Pharmacy had previously designated the intern program as a prerequisite requirement for professional registration as a pharmacist practitioner. To cite one example, the Maryland Board of Pharmacy now officially accepts the clerkship experience of pharmacy students at the University of Maryland School of Pharmacy as fully meeting internship requirements necessary for licensure in the State of Maryland.

Changing Goals

Most men and women who graduate from schools of pharmacy pursue careers within the profession. However, a small percentage of pharmacy graduates change objectives while finishing degrees or upon graduation. To the credit of pharmacy education, those who

change goals do so with relative ease while using pharmacy experience to their advantage. Nearly all graduates, whether they intend to enter pharmacy or not, take the licensure examination so the right to practice legally is ensured. Those with newfound goals that require additional collegiate study can offset expenses by working as pharmacists, even if employed part-time.

Graduates who change goals fall into two categories. The first group consists of students who intended to become pharmacists but lost motivation during school due to growing interest in other fields. The other group is "second-choice" entrants who enrolled because of inability to gain admission to other health-career schools, such as medicine or dentistry, and graduate as pharmacists but with those original motivations intact. This is not true of all second-choice entrants, for many sing the praises of pharmacy after exposure to the curriculum and assume the role of born pharmacists. Neither group can be faulted and, in fact, should be admired for having the patience, strength, and determination to resist compromise in the pursuit of individual endeavors.

Hundreds of pharmacy graduates have become attorneys. The pharmacy graduate who becomes a lawyer has an in-depth understanding of two professions and is uniquely qualified to litigate matters involving drugs, malpractice, bioethics, Medicare/Medicaid, and health maintenance groups. The restructuring of the health-care industry has resulted in a burgeoning demand for lawyers who specialize in regulatory powers that are driving the health-care delivery system. There is a need for experts who understand managed-care organizations, long-term care entities, hospital management, antitrust law, patients' rights, employee benefits, federal/state health programs, and countless other aspects of health matters and their legal ramifications. Three groups of attorneys

who now cater specifically to problems related to legal aspects of health care are:

National Health Lawyers Association
1120 Connecticut Avenue NW, Suite 350
Washington, D.C. 20036

American Academy of Hospital Attorneys
840 North Lake Shore Drive
Chicago, Illinois 60611

American Health Lawyers Association
1025 Connecticut Avenue NW, Suite 600
Washington, D.C. 20036

It is apropos that, in addition to its six-year doctor of pharmacy program, Drake University's (Iowa) College of Pharmacy offers a unique study program that combines a doctor of jurisprudence degree with the doctor of pharmacy degree. The combined pharmacy and law degrees program allows completion of both separate degrees in eight years through joint cooperation with the Drake Law School.

Some graduate pharmacists who enter conventional and osteopathic medicine changed motivation due to experiences encountered, and some are second-choice entrants who never lost the desire to become physicians. Pharmacists who become physicians remain excellent friends of pharmacy because of their understanding of the field. Smaller numbers of pharmacists turn to dentistry, podiatry, or optometry; and the same can be said of these health professionals, who never forget their backgrounds in pharmacy.

Some pharmacy graduates become successful science teachers in public and private school systems. Pharmacists have been known

to gain certification as teachers through additional study and the earning of master of education degrees. Pharmacists have also gained entry to marketing and finance fields by earning graduate degrees in business administration. The versatility of the pharmacy degree makes it easy for graduates to shift gears toward other career goals. Vistas are limited only by individual desire and ambition.

Pharmacy schools are not premedical, predental, or teachers colleges, nor are applicants with these objectives welcomed as students. Graduates who decide to pursue avenues outside of pharmacy receive the guidance and support of professors and administrators in schools of pharmacy who do everything possible to assist them with the realization of career ambitions. Pharmacy graduates who are lost to other professions always remain allies of pharmacy because they are pharmacists, whether they practice or not. Those who leave the profession to pursue other interests enhance the importance and value of pharmacists who remain as practitioners. The majority of pharmacy's graduates assume positions of responsibility within the profession and contribute valuable services to society.

6

GRADUATE STUDY PROGRAMS IN PHARMACY

UNDERGRADUATE STUDY PROGRAMS are designed to impart basic knowledge to students and culminate with the awarding of the bachelor of arts degree (indicating broad knowledge within arts, humanities, or social sciences) or bachelor of science degree (indicating broad knowledge within natural sciences, mathematics, or technology). The graduate student in any field is in a program of study at an institution of higher education that leads to a degree more advanced than the baccalaureate, such as the professional doctorate degree. Professional doctorate programs are designed to prepare students for entrance to professional practice and culminate with the awarding of degrees in specialized areas, for example, O.D. (Doctor of Optometry), D.P.M. (Doctor of Podiatric Medicine), M.D. (Doctor of Medicine), D.D.S. (Doctor of Dental Surgery), J.D. (Doctor of Jurisprudence), D.V.M. (Doctor of Veterinary Medicine), and Pharm.D. (Doctor of Pharmacy).

The Graduate Degree

Graduate study programs are distinguished from undergraduate and professional study programs by their difficulty and objectives. Superior students pursue graduate studies so they can make significant contributions through research and/or gain the intellectual development and academic discipline essential to specific career goals. Graduate degrees prepare people for careers involving creative scholarship and research, intellectual problem solving, and recognition and understanding of issues. The need for productive, original, and creative personnel is especially great in health care, government, business, higher education, and industry.

Graduate Student Profile

Graduates of pharmacy schools who do not wish to become practitioners may need credentials beyond the entry degrees of pharmacy. Academic careers in pharmacy, industrial research and management positions, health-system practice, and executive careers in government and business are some of the occupational opportunities that will be enhanced by receipt of master of science (M.S.) and/or doctor of philosophy (Ph.D.) degrees.

In 2001, according to statistics from the American Association of Colleges of Pharmacy (aacp.org), approximately 77 percent of the eighty-three schools of pharmacy in the United States administered programs in graduate education. At this writing, sixty-four pharmacy schools have students enrolled in various master of science and/or doctor of philosophy degree programs. In academic year 1999–2000, there were 3,084 graduate students enrolled in pharmacy schools working toward master of science and/or doc-

tor of philosophy degrees. About 50 percent of all graduate students have baccalaureate degrees in pharmacy, and the balance hold baccalaureates in other disciplines such as biology and chemistry. Women account for roughly 48 percent of all graduate students in pharmacy schools (60.5 percent of women received master's degrees and 43.7 percent of women received doctor of philosophy degrees). Foreign graduate students represent about 47 percent of total enrollments (33 percent of foreign students received master's degrees and 44 percent received doctor of philosophy degrees).

In fall 2001, 23 percent of full-time graduate students were master's candidates and 77 percent candidates for doctor of philosophy degrees. Of the 820 students enrolled in full-time master of science degree programs in fall 2001, Asian-Americans accounted for 10 percent of the enrollees, African-Americans for 5.6 percent, and Hispanic-Americans for 3.9 percent. Of the 2,264 students enrolled full-time in schools of pharmacy as candidates for doctor of philosophy degrees, Asian-Americans accounted for 14.4 percent, African-Americans for 4 percent, and Hispanic-Americans for 1.6 percent.

Upon entering the final year of study in a professional degree program in pharmacy, a student should have some inkling whether he or she will pursue graduate studies. The student with an outstanding academic record may be inclined to continue studies toward higher degrees. Students who have elected research-type courses during the professional program may be motivated toward graduate study. Professors will often take notice of excellent students and encourage them to consider postgraduate work. There are also some students in pharmacy schools who have determined early on that their futures require graduate study to fulfill creative career objectives.

Graduate Study Admissions

The high school transcript is an important credential in gaining admission to community colleges, junior colleges, and liberal arts institutions. However, once a student is admitted for preprofessional studies, the preprofessional college transcript is the credential that serves as entrée to a school of pharmacy for completion of the first professional degree. If the student decides to pursue a graduate program, it is the baccalaureate transcript that is an important qualifying credential in the application process. To be admitted to any graduate program in the pharmaceutical sciences, a student must demonstrate proof that a bachelor's degree or its equivalent has been earned from an accredited institution.

Applicants to graduate schools are evaluated on several criteria. The grade point average of the applicant's baccalaureate transcript must be superior. Grade point averages required for admission to graduate programs will vary from one school to another, but most schools demand no less than a 2.8 grade point average (on a 4.0 scale) and prefer a 3.0 (B average) or better for all undergraduate work. Some graduate schools receive so many applications that their admissions committees may increase the minimum average to 3.3 (B+) or better.

Just as Scholastic Aptitude Tests (SATs) are required for admission to undergraduate colleges, there is a special test designed for graduate admissions called the Graduate Record Examination (GRE). The GRE is a three-hour examination designed to yield separate scores for verbal, quantitative, and analytical abilities at the graduate level of study. Admissions officers use it to supplement undergraduate records and other indicators of applicants' potential for graduate study. The GRE is administered by the Educational Testing Service (ETS), Princeton, New Jersey, each year to about

five hundred thousand students at more than 250 different test centers including colleges, universities, and at Sylvan Learning Centers throughout the United States. You can schedule a test session by calling the Sylvan Candidate Services Call Center at (800) GRE-CALL or you can register online at gre.org. General information about the GRE can be obtained by calling the ETS at (609) 771-7670. The charge for taking the computer version of the GRE is $99, but students gain flexibility of time and location and now receive test results almost instantly, instead of the four to five weeks it formerly took to get scores by mail. The former version taken on paper with a No. 2 pencil is scheduled only several times a year, whereas the computer version may be taken any day of any week by appointment.

The Minority Graduate Student Locater Service was developed by the Educational Testing Service at the request of the Graduate Record Examinations Board for the purpose of increasing graduate school opportunities for minority students. The service provides a way for participating institutions to identify minority students who are interested in graduate education. Registration for the locater service is not an application for admission to any graduate school and requires no fee. American minority students now constitute more than 6 percent of graduate students in schools of pharmacy.

Application for admission to a graduate program should be accomplished with ease because of the student's previous experiences in applying to undergraduate and/or professional schools. Ideally application should be made about one year prior to the proposed date of admission to meet all deadline requirements involving submission of transcripts from previously attended colleges, Graduate Record Examination scores, and letters of recommendation.

Some schools may require interviews; and foreign students will have to submit scores for the Test of English as a Foreign Language (TOEFL), which is also administered periodically by the Educational Testing Service.

Programs in Graduate Study

Graduate programs in schools of pharmacy fall into five disciplinary categories:

1. Pharmaceutics/pharmacy
2. Pharmacy practice
3. Pharmaceutical chemistry/pharmacognosy
4. Pharmacology
5. Social and administrative sciences

In fall 2001 the highest number of master in science (M.S.) enrollees (31.7 percent) were majors in the discipline of pharmaceutics/pharmacy, as were enrollees at the doctoral level (36.5 percent).

Major subjects within pharmaceutics/pharmacy include areas of product development, sterile products, veterinary pharmacy, cosmetology, and industrial pharmaceutics. Courses in pharmacy practice encompass health systems, hospital practice, drug information, epidemiology and demography, clinical pharmacy, and administrative communication. Enrollees majoring in pharmaceutical chemistry/pharmacognosy find courses related to medicinal chemistry, natural product chemistry, polymeric materials, mass spectrometry, and techniques of chromatography, as part of a structured program. Pharmacology majors would select from courses such as toxicology, pharmacodynamics and drug screening, psychopharmacology, ter-

atology, and chemical pharmacology. The discipline of social and administrative sciences entails courses such as drug abuse, computer validation, pharmaceutical economics, jurisprudence, regulatory and policy formulation, and health-care administration.

Reading descriptions of graduate programs in college bulletins and conferences with faculty members are essential to students deciding upon major areas of study. Those entering graduate programs are academically mature students who, at least, have completed baccalaureate degrees. They have developed interests and require some guidance from college counselors to finalize their graduate programs by selecting appropriate courses and research projects.

Master of Science Degree

A master of science graduate program is designed for students wishing to terminate study with this degree as well as for those who ultimately plan to continue toward a doctor of philosophy degree. Most institutions require completion of thirty semester hours of graduate study, which may or may not include a thesis. A thesis consists of a written report describing an original contribution in some area of research. The thesis counts as six semester hours of credit. If a thesis is required, that particular master's program must also consist of twenty-four semester hours of appropriate advanced course work. Candidates for M.S. degrees must sometimes demonstrate proficiency in a foreign language. Some programs require students to pass comprehensive oral or written examinations. Some programs replace the thesis and language requirements with written reports on field experiences but require more than thirty semester hour credits. Requirements will vary depending on the major area of study and the policies of the school's graduate committee.

Doctor of Philosophy Degree

The doctor of philosophy degree is the highest degree attainable in any field of study and represents the zenith of achievement in preparation for research and scholarship. The recipient of a doctor of philosophy degree has been formally recognized by the graduate body of a university as a scholar of the highest order in a particular discipline. Individuals may receive the Ph.D. in chemistry, biology, engineering, education, and numerous other fields, including philosophy. The word *philosophy* refers to rational investigation and critical study of the truths, principles, and concepts of any branch of knowledge, especially with a view to improving or reconstituting that branch of knowledge. Graduate pharmacy students may earn Ph.D.s in areas of pharmacy practice, pharmacology, pharmaceutical chemistry, pharmaceutics, and administrative sciences.

Requirements for the Ph.D. degree are stringent in comparison to those for the M.S. degree. To earn the Ph.D., students must:

1. Complete thirty semester hours of course work beyond those required for the M.S. degree
2. Demonstrate reading knowledge of two foreign languages
3. Pass an oral qualifying examination
4. Pass an oral and written comprehensive examination
5. Submit an acceptable thesis
6. Pass a final oral examination

Completion of a master of science degree is not usually prerequisite for entering a Ph.D. program, but the student without the M.S. must complete sixty semester hours of course work. As a rule, graduate students transfer thirty semester hours of course work from the M.S. degree as part of the Ph.D. course requirement.

These rigid requirements indicate that it takes considerable time to earn a Ph.D. degree. The zealous student may be able to complete the degree in a five-year period that includes the two-year study program for the M.S. degree. It isn't unusual for students to take longer than five years to meet requirements for the Ph.D. degree. Graduate schools sometimes place limits on the amount of time available for earning a Ph.D. degree. Academic requirements vary from one institution to another as do time limitations. The high school student who reads about graduate studies may believe that this accomplishment is far out of reach. Not so! Preparation for graduate study begins in secondary school and is strengthened in an undergraduate institution. The transition from high school freshman to college senior to graduate student is an academic metamorphosis that occurs when good students are motivated and dedicated to self-improvement and the wonder of knowledge. Graduate degrees are the keys to careers of invention and discovery.

Financial Aid

Full-time graduate students have more sources of financial support available to them than do part-time graduate students. It is also true that a greater percentage of full-time doctor of philosophy students receive stipends than do full-time master of science students. Sources of financial aid for graduate students include government grants and loans, private foundations, stipends, university teaching fellowships, research assistantships, and residence assistantships.

At the forefront with abundant support for graduate pharmacy students is the American Foundation for Pharmaceutical Education (afpenet.org), which is supported by pharmacy associations and the pharmaceutical industry. Since 1942 the foundation has been a vital link between pharmaceutical education and the vast industrial phar-

maceutical community that includes drug manufacturers and wholesalers, chain drugstore firms, publishers, and consultant agencies. Since 1944 the AFPE has funded more than sixteen hundred Ph.D. candidates in schools of pharmacy with fellowships, scholarships, and postdoctoral fellowships worth more than $8 million. In the 2000–2001 academic year, the AFPE awarded $794,000 in scholarships, fellowships, and grants. Information regarding application for AFPE funds is available from the dean's office of any American pharmacy school with a graduate program leading to the doctor of philosophy (Ph.D.) degree.

Many universities sponsor teaching fellowships for Ph.D. candidates and offer tuition benefits and stipends ranging from $14,000 to $16,000 per year in exchange for limited contact teaching hours. Graduate assistantships in pharmacy are also available to M.S. and Ph.D. students in exchange for twelve hours of student contact per week in various laboratories. For assisting in laboratory instruction, graduate assistants receive tuition remission plus stipends ranging from $1,200 to $1,600 per month. A limited number of government fellowships through the National Science Foundation offer annual stipends of $10,000 in addition to full tuition. You can also obtain a detailed list of fellowships offered by various corporations and organizations at aphanet.org/students/fellowships.

Graduate schools welcome qualified students seeking master of science and/or doctor of philosophy degrees and assist in every way with the provision of financial support. The presence of graduate students on the campus of a pharmacy school creates an academically stimulating environment and provides fresh manpower for limited undergraduate teaching and laboratory instruction. Financial support, in addition to tuition remission, is one way that pharmacy schools attract outstanding graduate students. However, the most important attraction is outstanding graduate programs monitored by prestigious professors.

7

HEALTH-SYSTEM PHARMACISTS

HEALTH-SYSTEM PHARMACISTS are qualified men and women engaged as pharmacist-practitioners who perform their duties in environments other than community pharmacies. The descriptive term *health-system pharmacist* made its debut in the early 1990s, thanks to the fracture of conventional pharmacy practice, and it gained wide acceptance when the American Society of Hospital Pharmacists officially changed its name to the American Society of Health-System Pharmacists on January 1, 1995. Health-system pharmacists accomplish their drug dispensing and counseling functions in various settings such as hospital pharmacies, hospital wards and rooms, and hospital emergency receiving departments. They also work in other settings that can include long-term care facilities, hospices for the terminally ill, health maintenance organizations, nursing homes, apartment complexes for retirees, and home health-care environments.

The United States Department of Labor's "Career Guide to Industries" (Bulletin 2453) states that "cost containment in health

care is a recurring theme, played out in the growing emphasis on providing services on a less costly outpatient, ambulatory basis; limiting unnecessary or low-priority services; and contracting out of services by hospitals." Enrollments in health maintenance organizations (HMOs) and preferred provider organizations (PPOs) continue to grow rapidly. Comprehensive coverage must control health insurance costs by emphasizing preventive care. Population of people aged eighty-five and older will grow faster than the total population, as will the demand for home health-care and nursing and personal care. As the baby boom generation ages, the incidence of stroke and heart disease will increase. In addition, medical group practice will become larger and more complex and will require more managerial and support workers.

Personnel Demand

The demand for the services of health-system pharmacists will increase through the year 2005 as pharmacists consult more and become more actively involved in patient drug therapy decision making. Other factors likely to increase personnel demand include the likelihood of scientific advances that will produce more products, the new developments in administering medications, the increasingly sophisticated consumer who will seek more information about drugs, and the continuing growth of an older population.

The diversity, flexibility, and versatility demonstrated by today's pharmacy practitioner must be attributed to the experiences and wisdom gained through the superb curricula designed by pharmacy educators. Fortunately for the public, pharmacy graduates are well armed with scientific, behavioral, and professional ammunition that allows them to move freely among the complex spaces that constitute the many arenas of pharmaceutical health care.

Dr. John A. Gans, Executive Vice President of the American Pharmaceutical Association, stated:

> In the future, Americans are going to become involved in their own healthcare even more than they are today. Self-care will become commonplace, and pharmacists will play a growing role in helping patients to safely and effectively choose and utilize self-medication. It was not long ago when students who selected pharmacy as a career had very few options upon graduation as to where and how they would practice their profession. Pharmacy was practiced almost exclusively in three places—the independent community pharmacy, the chain pharmacy, and the hospital pharmacy. Today that has changed dramatically. As the profession of pharmacy has become more sophisticated, specialized areas of pharmacy practice have evolved, and even more will emerge in the future.

The Home Health-Care Pharmacist

Home health care is the fastest growing part of Medicare as an increasing number of elderly invalids and shut-ins seek to receive nursing care, physical therapy, assistance with dressing and bathing, and drug therapy in their homes. Home visits by professionals exploded and increased from 31 million visits in 1984 to 824 million visits in 2002 (U.S. Center for Health Statistics).

Home health-care firms have greatly expanded their services and staff to include, beyond physicians, personnel such as nurses, physical and occupational therapists, social workers, respiratory technicians, and pharmacists. Pharmacists play an important role in home health care because they recommend therapy regimens, request blood testing when necessary, consult with doctors regarding patient progress, and monitor drug programs of individuals. It is understandable that patients would rather be at home than in

institutions. It is not surprising that patients recuperate more quickly in a home setting, which automatically reduces costs of treatment by an estimated 50 percent according to some insurance companies.

According to statistics from the U.S. Department of Labor, approximately 30 percent of all pharmacists work in the health services sector—hospitals, health maintenance organizations (HMOs), clinics, home health-care services, nursing homes, and federal government facilities.

The Emergency Department Pharmacist

In 1999 more than 102 million Americans went to the emergency rooms of hospitals (U.S. Center for Health Statistics). However, over 50 percent of those visits were for relatively minor health problems including sprained ankles, sore throats, common colds, and cuts and bruises. When emergencies involve complex drug interactions, drug overdoses, drug/disease incompatibilities, drug side effects, drug-related illness, and dosage and drug decisions, the presence and expertise of a pharmacist is invaluable to the professional team of a hospital emergency department (ED).

Emergency departments have slow times and fast times, depending upon the day of the week, the hour of the day, the location of the hospital, and the population size of the city or town. Large metropolitan cities provide more action in emergency departments, so it is unlikely that ED pharmacists would be found around-the-clock in the receiving departments of small, rural hospitals. Nevertheless, the role of the pharmacist in EDs of major hospital centers continues to gain acceptance and approval of emergency physicians and hospital administrators because of apparent economic and therapeutic advantages.

The Mail-Order Pharmacist

A mail-order pharmacy is an establishment that fills a prescription, as directed by a physician, and then mails the prescribed drug directly to the residence of the patient. Mail-order pharmacies have proliferated since the Veterans Administration instituted a program in 1946. The American Association of Retired Persons began its mail pharmacy service for members in 1959. It wasn't until the early 1980s that mail-order pharmacies took off with a vengeance. One mail-service pharmacy had sales of $100 million in 1981, reached $5 billion in sales in 1993, and exceeded $20 billion in sales by the year 2000. Another mail-service pharmacy began operating in 1983 and by 1995 was dispensing thirty million prescriptions annually to individuals who held membership in various unions and insurance carriers or were employed by participating corporations.

The 2.8 billion prescriptions dispensed by community pharmacies in 2000 represented more than 70 percent of dispensed prescriptions in the United States. Mail-order pharmacies accounted for about 12 percent of total prescription sales, or roughly 389 million prescriptions. To considerable extent, mail-order pharmacies were instrumental in the formation of pharmacy benefit managers (PBMs), which now contain pharmacy benefits for about half of all insured people in the United States. PBMs market their services to insurance companies, Medicaid, and health maintenance organizations as well as corporations. Pharmacists are employed by PBMs because of their knowledge of drugs and their management skills.

Mail-order outlets may charge less for their services for a number of reasons. These include less overhead; the issuance of ninety-day supplies of maintenance drugs; the use of "closed" formularies that restrict inclusion of new and expensive drugs; the implemen-

tation of therapeutic substitution, whereby drugs of the same pharmacologic action are interchanged; and generic substitution, whereby a tried-and-true brand name is replaced with a generic copy.

It requires the services of many pharmacists and pharmacy technicians to dispense and mail more than 389 million prescriptions annually, and the law requires that the process take place under the supervision of pharmacists. There is no face-to-face communication with clients. Patients may have to wait ten days to two weeks for receipt of medications, especially with first-time orders. It is doubtful that many modern pharmacists would engage in the practice of mail-order pharmacy because there would be little opportunity to put their vast insights and knowledge to use. Some pharmacists who settle into the practice of mail-order pharmacy are semiretired or retired practitioners.

The Hospital Pharmacist

America's health-service industry is one of the largest in the country. It consists of 432,000 establishments and employs more than eleven million people, which by the year 2010 is projected to grow by 25 percent and add 2.75 million employees—more than any other industry. The aforementioned establishments consist of 50 percent doctors' offices, 25 percent dental offices, and just 2 percent hospitals, although hospitals employ more than half (51.2 percent) of all health personnel.

The health-service revolution now in progress is taking its toll on the health of the hospital system in America. Changes in the treatment of the sick and ailing are having a profound effect on hospital policies, as reflected in the following statistics. The Labor Department notes that in 1990 hospitals were adding about ten

thousand positions per month, whereas during 1994 there was virtually no job growth in American hospitals. In 1987 there were 34.4 million people admitted to hospitals, but by 1993 only 30.7 million were admitted and the length of stay also declined. The American Hospital Association reports that between 1983 and 1993 urban and rural community hospitals all experienced a reduction in beds and a decline in admissions. In 1987 America's hospitals had 1,267,000 beds but by 1993 the number had declined to 1,033,827 beds. In 1999 the number of beds decreased to 994,000. In 1987 there were 6,821 general hospitals in the United States, but by 1999 the number had shrunk to 5,890. What *is* increasing is the number of outpatients, which went from 311 million in 1987 to 573 million in 1999 (*Statistical Abstracts of the United States, 2001*).

Profit margins of hospitals have declined or stagnated, increasing the pressure to reduce costs. Hospitals did this by discharging patients sooner; performing more outpatient surgery, thereby eliminating overnight care; closing underused facilities; eliminating staff and administrative positions; and contracting out-of-hospital services with for-profit agencies that franchised emergency department personnel, laboratory services, and auxiliary prescription providers.

Add to these facts the amazing contributions of "wonder" drugs that have kept patients out of hospitals. ACE inhibitor drugs for congestive heart failure avoided $9,000 in costs per patient in hospitalization fees over a three-year period and saved Americans with heart failure about $2 billion per year. Prior to the use of H2 antagonist drugs for ulcer therapy in 1977, there were ninety-seven thousand ulcer operations performed each year. By 1987, surgeries dropped to about nineteen thousand, thereby replacing the $28,000 cost for surgery and care with the annual cost of $900 per patient,

per year, for drug therapy. Lastly, to cite a third example of count-less people avoiding hospital confinement, the annual cost for treating schizophrenia with drugs is $4,500 compared to $73,000 a year for treatment in a state mental institution.

As a result of hospital downsizing, the number of pharmacists working in hospital environments has proportionally declined. Personnel directors of hospitals prefer that pharmacists either hold doctor of pharmacy degrees or satisfactorily complete one of the more than four hundred residency programs in hospital pharmacy following graduation from a school of pharmacy. Pharmacists who earn master of science degrees in social and administrative sciences are also welcomed into some hospital settings.

Residency Programs in Hospital Pharmacy

Hospitals prepare announcements of their residency programs, mail them to schools of pharmacy, and place ads in publications, and students apply prior to graduation as pharmacists. These one-year residency programs consist of two thousand hours of structured and unstructured instruction. The programs pay residents while they are earning certification for future employment as hospital pharmacists. Candidates must be registered pharmacists.

A Typical Residency Program

At least 400 hours are devoted to inpatient, outpatient, and general dispensing techniques. The formulation, preparation, and manufacturing of nonsterile and sterile dosage forms occupy at least 200 hours of training. Pediatric, geriatric, ophthalmological, and dermatological medications are just some of the dosage classes that require specific understanding in their preparation and use. Hospital pharmacy administration engages the resident for a minimum

of 200 hours during the year. Familiarity with drug information services is achieved with 100 hours of training. Assignments to various nursing units provide 100 hours of background in clinical services, including the general care of patients. Lecturers, seminars, and conferences, including interdisciplinary programs attended by nurses, doctors, administrators, and pharmacists, constitute 100 hours of credit. Interdepartmental activities are introduced via communication with nursing supervisors, therapy administrators, dieticians, departmental chairpersons, and executives during 100 hours of visits and observation. A balance of 800 hours is devoted to unstructured pharmacy services, which may include a written project selected with approval of the residency director.

Approach to Hospital Pharmacy

The question arises how to best prepare for a career in hospital pharmacy practice. There are thousands of successful, prominent hospital pharmacists with diverse educational backgrounds. Some achieved their positions through residency programs, others with graduate degrees, and some with doctor of pharmacy diplomas. The student deciding upon a pathway toward hospital pharmacy practice must take an introspective approach through self-evaluation of disposition and objectives. Communication with others who have experienced the educational programs described is helpful, as is reading literature that outlines residencies, graduate programs, and doctor of pharmacy curricula. The specialty aimed for within hospital pharmacy practice will play a role in the student's decision if he or she knows with certainty what that goal is.

Though it is difficult to accomplish, some pharmacists get hospital pharmacy jobs right out of college with baccalaureate in pharmacy degrees and without undergoing residencies or graduate study.

Clinical clerkships in the pharmacy program bring students into hospital pharmacies, and some outstanding students create favorable impressions that lead to future employment. The pharmacist holding the baccalaureate in pharmacy degree who secures a hospital position may be confined to limited responsibilities, such as outpatient dispensing, but such work may be fulfilling and the salary satisfactory. A disadvantage is that learning on the job has its limitation, and promotions will not come easily without credentials beyond the entry-level degree in pharmacy. There are brilliant chief pharmacists whose credentials are limited to baccalaureate degrees, but these men and women studied pharmacy before advanced hospital instructional programs were available, and their years of experience, continuing education, and practical wisdom compensate for what is now considered a shortcoming.

Pharmacists who complete graduate programs will not necessarily make better hospital pharmacists than those who complete residency programs or doctor of pharmacy degrees. Dedication, enthusiasm, honesty, communication, patience, and integrity play a significant part, for it is the individual's human spirit that provides the chemistry of success in a hospital pharmacy career.

Job Benefits

A recent salary survey (available at allied-physicians.com) provides current income statistics for health-system pharmacists. The median base salary for a hospital pharmacist was $65,000. The average salary for a pharmacist employed by a health maintenance organization (HMO) was $75,000. Pharmacists who, over the years, are promoted to chief executive officers (CEOs) and manage entire health facilities command even more substantial incomes.

Health-system pharmacists also receive fringe benefits not reflected in salaries. Benefits include paid vacations, maternity and sick leaves, pension programs, health and life insurance, free tuition for continuing education courses, and job protection in the form of union affiliation.

The environment enjoyed by health-system pharmacists is price-less! Relationships with other health professionals are stimulating, and the accomplishments of practice provide self-gratification and a well-defined sense of purpose. Health-care delivery in a complex institution presents intriguing challenges to pharmacy practition-ers whose services are essential to smooth, successful patient care.

8

COMMUNITY PHARMACY

PHARMACY GRADUATES WHO decide to specialize in community practice have selected the most taxing and exciting of all undertakings within the profession. No other specialty in pharmacy requires as many demanding physical and mental qualifications as does community pharmacy practice. Community pharmacists encounter more people in a single day than do any other health practitioners, and they must be prepared for the reactions of each visitor to the pharmacy. Because of their availability to the public, who need not make appointments for consultation, pharmacists must offer concise, correct information to patients every day. As you can see, this field of pharmacy consistently demands broad general knowledge, tact, interpersonal skills, administrative ability, economic know-how, and stamina on the part of its participants.

Practicing community pharmacy requires physical endurance because the pharmacist stands and walks a great deal each day. Talking, observing, and listening are fundamental components of community practice as the pharmacist serves a stream of patients

bearing prescriptions and buying over-the-counter health aids. Unpredictable telephone calls from physicians and patients occupy pharmacists as they relay information and accept instructions from other practitioners. Pharmacists spend the day maneuvering through prescription laboratories, storerooms, sales areas, offices, and telephone spaces.

Other specialties in pharmacy do not require the same dexterity or exposure to unpredictable elements. Researchers work quietly within laboratories and receive fewer phone calls and visitors, as contemplation is essential to discovery and invention. Pharmacy professors have an audience of students and communicate with associates while devoting time to desk work. Pharmaceutical sales representatives visit physicians and pharmacists and have relatively predictable information exchanges and schedules. Administrators in library research, public relations, pharmacy associations, industrial management, marketing, government service, and education may spend considerable time doing paperwork and communicating predictably with a limited number of peers. Hospital pharmacists require the same agility as community pharmacists, but they don't confront the public to the same extent or participate in the sale of nonprescription drugs and products. All of the specialties require unique skills and talents and challenge their participants. However, most pharmacists agree that community practice remains as the frontier of pharmacy. Community pharmacists need patience, poise, perception, knowledge, endurance, and sensitivity to provide the community-at-large with expert drug services.

Licensure and Reciprocity

Graduates of schools of pharmacy who prepare and dispense prescriptions and provide health services to the public are practition-

ers of pharmacy. As such they must meet licensure requirements defined by laws of the state(s) in which they practice. Other specialists in pharmacy, such as researchers, journalists, pharmacy professors, pharmaceutical sales representatives, and administrators need not be licensed to perform their duties. However, nearly all graduates seek licensure upon graduation from a school of pharmacy because they take pride in the right to practice should the occasion arise. Some pharmacy graduates who enter nonpractice areas enjoy gaining renewed licenses; some practice pharmacy part-time.

Licensure for pharmacists in all jurisdictions consists of: presentation of graduation credentials from a school of pharmacy, proof of clerkship or internship, payment of the examination fee to the state, and successful passing of the examination. All states except California now administer licensing examinations under the auspices of the National Association of Boards of Pharmacy (NABP).

Carmen A. Catizone, Executive Director/Secretary of the National Association of Boards of Pharmacy, noted that the "regulation of pharmacy is a responsibility that members of the state boards of pharmacy take very seriously. While pharmacy professionals are licensed only after demonstrating that they possess the necessary knowledge, skill, and ability to practice safely, the licensure requirement also motivates these individuals to retain their strong commitment to the profession and the protection of the public health and well-being."

Because of the cooperative spirit among state boards of pharmacy and the excellent coordinative efforts of the National Association of Boards of Pharmacy, registered pharmacists may move and gain licensure in a new state with relative ease. This mutual exchange policy is referred to as *reciprocity* and, though cooperating states differ in requirements, the principle of extending privi-

leges of practice is characteristic of all except California and Florida. To practice in California or Florida, the pharmacist who is previously registered in another state must take another licensing examination. To move among the remaining forty-eight states, the registered pharmacist may have to take a jurisprudence test to guarantee familiarity with local laws or have been registered elsewhere for at least one year. Pharmacists move about for health reasons, preference of climate, job opportunities, and other personal motives; but wherever pharmacists practice, there are licensure requirements. Shifts in population growth and the number of pharmacies within a state also are factors that account for the transfer of pharmacists from one state to another. Statistics from the National Association of Boards of Pharmacy (nabp.net) indicate that approximately fifty-eight hundred pharmacists moved from one state to another in 2001.

United States and Canada Validate New Licensing Exam

In 1996 the Executive Committee of the National Association of Boards of Pharmacy implemented the North American Pharmacy Licensing Examination (NAPLEX). In line with directives established by its membership, NABP worked cooperatively with representatives from the Pharmacy Examining Board of Canada (PEBC) and the National Association of Pharmacy Regulatory Authorities (NAPRA) toward the development of a licensing exam that integrated U.S. and Canadian competency evaluations.

The focus of NAPLEX is on drug therapy. Three overall competency areas designate 50 percent of the test to managing drug therapy to optimize patient outcomes; 25 percent to ensuring the accurate preparation and dispensing of medications; and the remaining 25 percent to providing drug information and promot-

ing public health. Every U.S. state and Canadian province was represented in the validation survey's response data set, so that the respondents' demographics and practice data could be generalized with confidence to the North American population of licensed pharmacists. As a result of the NABP's efforts, pharmacy practice is one of the first professions to meet and exceed the expectations of the North American Free Trade Agreement (NAFTA).

The Prescription

The pharmacy graduate who receives a license to practice is now qualified to assume the role of a registered pharmacist. The community pharmacist may work in a privately owned pharmacy or in a chain pharmacy that is corporately owned. No matter the setting, it is the prescription that will occupy the greatest amount of the pharmacist's time. The prescription is an order, usually written, from a physician to a pharmacist that specifies the medication to be dispensed to a patient. The written prescription is usually handed to the patient by the doctor and presented by the patient to the pharmacist. Upon receiving the prescription, the pharmacist will observe the patient and scrutinize the prescription.

If the person delivering the prescription is the individual for whom the medication is intended, the pharmacist will observe the patient's weight, age, sex, and general appearance. Small though the prescription appears, it contains a great deal of information that is professionally interpreted by the pharmacist. Information on a prescription includes:

- Name of patient
- Address of patient

- Name and registration number of physician
- Address of physician
- Date of prescription
- Form of medication
- Name of medication
- Strength of medication
- Amount of medication
- Dosage of medication
- Administration method of medication
- Frequency and time to administer medication

Depending on the nature of the drug(s) and health of the patient, the pharmacist may need to provide advice or question the patient. It is in filling the prescription that the pharmacist's knowledge of pharmacology, medicinal chemistry, and biopharmaceutics comes into play. Although automation and computerization have a place in pharmacy, it is the pharmacist who applies the theory of these many sciences to determine the effectiveness of the prescription. The pharmacist checks the prescription for physical and chemical compatibility of ingredients, for safety and efficiency of dosage, and for legal requirements, among other factors.

Once the written prescription has been checked as noted, the pharmacist is ready to process the order. From the thousands of drugs manufactured in different forms and doses, the pharmacist collects the drug(s) called for by the prescription. Fortunately for patients and pharmacists, current drugs are manufactured in convenient dosage forms by the pharmaceutical industry and do not require complicated compounding procedures by pharmacists.

Once the pharmacist has selected the medication, it is again checked with the prescription order and appropriately packaged to meet storage and size requirements convenient to the patient. Con-

tainers may be bottles, boxes, jars, or vials; glass or plastic; transparent, opaque, or colored; dropper or pour bottles. After the drug has been packaged, it is labeled with the patient's name, doctor's name, date, prescription number, directions for administration, and any special cautionary instructions.

The pharmacist also records information such as the number assigned to the order (to coincide with the number on the label), date dispensed, price charged, and notes regarding any unusual procedures employed in its preparation. Before delivery of the finished package to the patient, the pharmacist once again confirms the ingredients and label information against the doctor's written order. Finally the prescription is considered in relation to state and federal laws.

The pharmacist now presents the finished prescription to the patient. At this time the pharmacist reads the label aloud to the patient and explains in detail any unusual procedures involved in using the medicine. The patient is given the opportunity to ask questions during this exchange. The patient leaves the pharmacy not only with a prescription, but also with the knowledge that a valuable service has been received.

Stimulating Challenges and Responsibilities

Considering all the responsibilities and duties of the practicing community pharmacist, there are only so many prescriptions that can be filled with precision in an allotted time span. A good part of the pharmacist's workload must be devoted to counseling, advising, and giving pharmaceutical care to consumers. In the state of California, pharmacists are no longer overwhelmed by the pressure of having to fill an excess number of prescriptions per hour. Recently the California Pharmacists Association set a maximum of fifteen pre-

scriptions per hour per pharmacist in its model employee pharmacist contract. National pharmacy associations have turned their attention to resolving the dilemma facing pharmacists throughout the nation. What are the guidelines for balancing the counseling and dispensing responsibilities of pharmacists, and how are they to be compensated for the multiple and diverse services provided to consumers?

To fill a single prescription, the pharmacist uses knowledge culled from pharmacology, medicinal chemistry, biopharmaceutics, mathematics, economics, law, behavioral science, clinical pharmacy, and management. The diversified education and experience of the pharmacist provide the confidence, ease, and performance that make a complex transaction seem simple.

In August 1995 Donna Shalala, Secretary of the Department of Health and Human Services, in "A Dose of Clear Directions for Rx Drug Users" (FDA), proposed that every prescription drug received by a consumer be accompanied by a leaflet of clear, concise information about the prescribed medication: "Working together and using today's computer technology, we can make prescription information more widely available, more understandable, and more relevant for each individual patient." The plan required pharmacists to provide a write-up on the side effects and/or dangers of drug combinations as well as other pertinent information to 75 percent of patients submitting new prescriptions by the year 2000, with an increase to 95 percent of consumers by the year 2006. The Food and Drug Administration proposed that pharmacists voluntarily offer comprehensive information on the more than thirty-three hundred drugs now available to patients. Failure to cooperate would result in mandatory compliance.

Recent statistics and surveys on the number of prescriptions dispensed by American community pharmacies indicate that the great-

est percentage of practitioner time is devoted to prescription processing. In 2000 more than 2.8 billion prescriptions were dispensed
in the United States. Private and chain pharmacies now annually
dispense ten prescriptions for every man, woman, and child in the
population. This does not include hospital pharmacy prescriptions
or drugs administered to confined institutional patients. Patients
paid pharmacists directly for approximately 35 percent of 2.8 billion prescriptions, and the remaining 65 percent was paid by third-
party payment programs such as federal and state government
plans, union benefit programs, private health insurance groups,
managed-care organizations, health maintenance organizations, corporations, and trusts.

According to the U.S. Census Bureau, the population of the
United States in 2000 was 281,421,906. Recent estimates indicate
that about 25 percent of Americans have no insurance coverage for
prescription drugs. The remaining 75 percent of Americans have
some form of drug coverage, although it is nearly always limited
with copayments or deductibles. In 2000 nearly 6 million elderly
Americans among Medicare's 39 million beneficiaries were enrollees
in health maintenance organizations (HMOs). Approximately 20
million persons received prescribed drugs under Medicaid in 1999.
In 2000 there were 78 million people enrolled in HMOs and an
additional 152 million members in managed-care organizations
(MCOs). Three of every four workers in the United States are
under the umbrella of some form of managed care that provides a
form of prescription drug coverage (*Health Care Financing Review*,
U.S. Centers for Medicare and Medicaid Services, 2000).

To cope with the financial risks of dealing with many third-party
payers for prescriptions, all community pharmacies now have computer systems that cost $10,000 and up, and some have satellite
links that, within seconds, confirm the patient's eligibility and other

parameters such as drugs covered, generic viability, and amount limitations. One chain of community pharmacies now deals with eight hundred different insurance plans. Jeffrey Greene, president of The Pharmacy Fund, a company that services community pharmacies with overnight cash for third-party accounts in exchange for a percentage fee, recently noted, "On any one day, the retail pharmacy industry is owed $1.8 billion in third-party receivables."

Administration and Management

In addition to processing prescriptions and communicating with patients, the pharmacist performs many administrative tasks. An inventory record of supplies must be maintained to ensure availability of prescription items and over-the-counter drugs. The environment of the pharmacy must be appealing, and this involves neat physical arrangements, clean floors and windows, uncluttered flow of foot traffic, comfortable room temperature, good lighting, and an available patient waiting area.

The pharmacist-owner has these and other managerial responsibilities too numerous to handle alone; therefore he or she must act as a personnel supervisor in hiring other pharmacists, porters, clerks, pharmacy technicians, accountants, deliverers, and other supportive employees. Engaging a staff necessitates instituting policies on employee benefits, pay scale, vacations, and sick leave.

The extent of administrative responsibility varies with the status of the practitioner. Pharmacist-owners are obviously more obligated to management than pharmacist-employees. Pharmacist-managers of chain pharmacies have greater responsibilities than assistant staff pharmacists. Management policies of pharmacy chains vary considerably, and in most instances, the pharmacist in charge performs only prescription services while a full-time nonpharmacist man-

ager is in charge of the complete establishment. Overseeing a large pharmacy involves many inconspicuous problems of management involving security systems, pilferage, accident liability, malpractice insurance, union negotiations, and detection of fraudulent prescriptions and bad checks. Good management is the glue that helps build the sound organizational structure so vital to a successful community pharmacy.

Pharmacy Aides and Pharmacy Technicians

Pharmacists are very busy professionals and nothing they do in the pharmacy is accomplished by rote. Every function of the pharmacist requires constant thought, reason, and contemplation. The nonstop demands upon the pharmacist beg for assistance from qualified helpers, and such support is often obtained from pharmacy aides and pharmacy technicians.

In 2000 there were fifty-seven thousand pharmacy aides employed in American pharmacies. Their duties included the mixing of some pharmaceuticals under the direction of pharmacists, the labeling and storage of supplies, and the cleaning of equipment and work areas. More than 80 percent were employed in retail pharmacies, either independently owned or part of a drugstore chain, department store, grocery store, or mass retailer. It is projected that by the year 2005, an additional fifteen thousand pharmacy aides will be employed in American pharmacies. Pharmacy aides gain their skills over at least twelve months of on-the-job training under the supervision of one or more registered pharmacists. Average hourly earnings of pharmacy aides were approximately $8.50 in 2000 (*Occupational Outlook Handbook, 2002–03*).

Pharmacy technicians differ from pharmacy aides in that they are assigned roles of greater responsibility because of their source

of training and/or certification through a valid credentialing process. Pharmacy technicians may earn associate degrees from technical schools or junior colleges. In 2000 there were 190,000 pharmacy technicians gainfully employed in community and institutional pharmacies throughout the country. Under the supervision and direction of a pharmacist, technicians are able to fill orders for unit doses and prepackaged pharmaceuticals and perform other related duties. These duties include keeping records of incoming drugs, storing merchandise in proper locations, and informing supervisors when inventory diminishes. Technicians are called upon to assist in the care and maintenance of equipment as well as supplies. It would be demeaning to a pharmacist if he or she were hired to merely perform the functions of a pharmacy aide or technician, which is why pharmacies engage such personnel in the overall management of a pharmacy facility. Median hourly earnings of pharmacy technicians in 2000 were $9.93 (*Occupational Outlook Handbook, 2002–03*).

Recent progress in this corner of pharmacy includes the formation of the Pharmacy Technician Certification Board (2215 Constitution Avenue NW, Washington, D.C. 20037, ptcb.org). This freestanding corporation was created by the American Pharmaceutical Association, the American Society of Health-System Pharmacists, the Illinois Council of Hospital Pharmacists, and the Michigan Pharmacists Association for the purpose of testing and licensing certified pharmacy technicians as well as formally defining the role of the technician in modern pharmacy. In addition to this innovation, the National Community Pharmacists Association and the National Association of Chain Drug Stores have developed a training manual for community pharmacy technicians, which is supported by an educational grant from Syntex Laboratories. The synergy of an authoritative training manual for pharmacy techni-

cians and the administration of a national certification examination to them will ultimately benefit the public as pharmacists gain more time for direct health-care counseling to patients.

Health Information Center

The community pharmacy is now established as a health information center with the pharmacist as the distributor of health education information to the community and to other health-care professionals. Health associations of every description ask community pharmacists to distribute pamphlets on specific diseases and their prevention and treatment. The pharmacist accommodates nonprofit national and local health associations by inserting their literature in shopping parcels and strategically arranging materials in places of client access. In this manner, pharmacists have disseminated information to millions of people about cancer, AIDS, heart disease, diabetes, glaucoma, venereal disease, alcoholism, nutrition, drug abuse, and poison prevention.

The pharmacist maintains drug reference materials including books, journals, update reports, files, formularies, subscription services, and phone numbers of poison centers and drug retrieval information centers. CD-ROM technology has made available to pharmacists instant drug information from some classic reference books including *Physicians' Desk Reference* (*PDR*), which illustrates in full color the many dosage forms of drugs along with vital information, and *Drug Facts*, which has pertinent information on more than twenty thousand drugs and six thousand over-the-counter products. Software updates on drug products are distributed quarterly rather than annually in word-on-paper formats. Physicians call upon pharmacists for drug information, recommendations on drug regimen planning, and specific drug therapy. Physicians increas-

ingly consult pharmacists regarding drug choices. The practice of medicine is primarily concerned with determining the nature and circumstances of diseased conditions, and it is difficult for physicians to keep abreast of thousands of prescription drugs available in multiple dosages and forms. Therefore, the pharmacist, as the acknowledged drug expert, is depended upon for counsel. This team approach to health care is expanding the role of the pharmacist as the authority on drug choice.

Pharmacists project an image of community service and are sought for membership on committees of charitable organizations, boards of health, and civic societies. Public and private schools invite pharmacists to participate in career forums, and community groups want to be addressed on health subjects such as drug abuse, contraception, and self-medication.

The Pharmacist: A Permanent Student

Though pharmacists are thought of as providers of knowledge, it may not be apparent that pharmacists are also perpetual students who must reinforce and augment their knowledge and skills to remain professionally competent. Learning is as precious to the professional survival of the pharmacist as rain and sun are to the survival of things that grow. The pharmacist keeps abreast of scientific and professional developments in pharmacy through both structured and nonstructured learning.

Nonstructured learning occurs informally as pharmacists communicate with professionals and patients about drug usage. It occurs as pharmaceutical sales representatives visit pharmacies to talk about their companies' new drug products and distribute literature. And nonstructured learning also occurs as pharmacists scan daily mail

advertisements from pharmaceutical manufacturers, computer firms, and supply houses.

Structured learning is planned and requires setting aside time to listen to informational tapes or carefully study scientific and professional journals. Pharmacists purchase textbooks and drug encyclopedias and subscribe to software reference services that provide updates of current information each month. Structured learning occurs when pharmacists attend continuing education (CE) courses sponsored by pharmacy schools or associations, drug manufacturers, and interdisciplinary professional groups. The range of subjects presented to pharmacists in continuing courses is sweeping. A random sampling of recent programs reveals that instruction has focused on subjects such as Alzheimer's disease, nutrition, AIDS, pain, pulmonary disease, hypertension, epilepsy, geriatrics, and diabetes mellitus.

Most state boards of pharmacy mandate that pharmacists annually complete specified continuing education units to gain licensure renewal. In most states with established CE legislation, pharmacists are required to annually master fifteen units of approved content to renew their licenses. The American Council on Pharmaceutical Education is the national agency for approval of providers of continuing pharmaceutical education.

Specialized Practices

Some community pharmacists have specialized practices that distinguish them from typical community or chain pharmacies. The apothecary is a pharmacy that concentrates on prescription services and convalescent care supplies and chooses to eliminate the sale of sundries and patent medicines. Apothecaries, staffed by pharma-

cists only, are often located in medical centers that house offices of physicians and dentists. Convalescent care supplies encompass medical/surgical aids, rehabilitation equipment, special garments and supports, ostomy supplies, and countless items required by patients with specific needs.

Some young pharmacy school graduates have the entrepreneurial drive to own their own pharmacies and ultimately achieve their goals. It takes considerable experience and investment to start an independent pharmacy that generates sales of $1.25 million annually, but many individuals have achieved this objective through hard work, savings, and determination. Retiring owners sometimes arrange for employee pharmacists to assume ownerships on terms that are fair and often unconventional. Wholesalers, contractors, and realtors often provide support and encouragement to the young, qualified professional who wishes to establish a new, independent pharmacy in a community in need of such services.

Corporate ownership of four or more pharmacies makes each member pharmacy a part of a "chain pharmacy." It is estimated that pharmacy chains in the United States generated sales of approximately $68 billion in 2001. There are approximately thirty-three thousand chain pharmacies in the United States representing about one-half of all community pharmacies, and these outlets provide challenging positions to more than 108,000 pharmacists (99,000 full-time), according to the National Association of Chain Drug Stores (nacds.org).

The National Council for Prescription Drug Programs, or NCPDP, estimates that the total number of pharmacies in the United States has remained relatively stable over the past ten years. Data indicate that independently owned pharmacies are being

replaced by chain pharmacies. Between 1991 and 2001, independent pharmacies in the United States declined by roughly ten thousand as chain pharmacies increased by approximately two thousand. Fierce competition in a volatile marketplace has taken its toll on small, independent pharmacies. Because of rapid openings and closings of pharmacies, takeovers of pharmacies, and construction of new community pharmacies, it is difficult to arrive at a statistic identifying the balance of chain and independent pharmacies in the United States. Upon reviewing statistics from various governmental and private sources, this author believes that there are approximately fifty-three thousand community pharmacies in the United States consisting of about thirty-three thousand chain pharmacies and twenty thousand independent pharmacies.

Pharmacy Practice Incentives

Practicing community pharmacists may be found in independent pharmacies, chain pharmacies, apothecaries, and other settings. Pharmacists are well rewarded for their services no matter where they are employed. It is conservatively estimated that approximately five thousand pharmacists withdraw from the profession each year due to retirement, health reasons, death, or miscellaneous causes. About eight thousand graduates emerge from pharmacy schools annually, and some choose to pursue nonpracticing careers such as postgraduate study, industry-related positions, teaching, or other specialty areas. Economics has been loosely defined as the "science of scarcity," and it is this factor, combined with educational qualifications, that commands excellent salaries for pharmacists. The making of a pharmacist requires at least five to six years of suc-

cessful higher education and the expenditure of energy and assets along the way. The value of the pharmacist is reflected in compensation for services.

An excellent survey in *Drug Topics* (2001) indicates that in 2000 pharmacists employed by independent pharmacies earned average total compensation of approximately $62,040 per year. As in all occupations, the salary of the pharmacist is influenced by experience, overtime income, benefits programs, managerial capacity, and geographical region. Pharmacists employed by chain drugstores command the higher income of approximately $71,486 per year. Pension programs, medical insurance, disability coverage, paid vacations, overtime income, profit sharing, bonuses, pregnancy and sick leaves, and employee discounts are benefits that most chains and many independent owners offer to employee pharmacists.

Days are never dull for pharmacists. An unending array of patients, professionals, drugs, and issues kaleidoscopically regroup with each passing moment. Understandably, during free time, pharmacists lead lives much apart from the busy realm of professional responsibilities. Pharmacists participate in political affairs and have won office as mayors, senators, and members of state and local legislatures. Pharmacists have gained recognition as authors, musicians, artists, photographers, and hobbyists. Men and women from a wide spectrum of age groups, ethnic origins, races, religions, and ideologies enjoy the life of the practicing pharmacist. They share a bond of professionalism and a proud, productive sense of dedication to human welfare. Do you have the enthusiasm, energy, and interest necessary to join this distinguished group?

9

Industrial Pharmacy

It is the innovative industrial segment of the American pharmaceutical community that fuels the fires of progress responsible for the research, production, and marketing of most prescription drugs, medical devices, and diagnostic products used throughout the world. Research and development (R&D) by America's pharmaceutical industry surpassed $42 billion in 2000.

Dimensions of Industry

In 2000 the U.S. pharmaceutical industry employed 320,000 persons (Bureau of Labor Statistics, 2002). These employees worked in production, manufacturing, and quality control; in sales and marketing; on medical research and development; and with distribution and countless administrative areas familiar only to those within the industry. It is difficult to estimate how many pharmacists are employed in the many areas of pharmaceutical industry

because some are not registered with state boards of pharmacy and thus are not counted in statistical surveys. It is estimated that at least six thousand registered pharmacists are employed by pharmaceutical industry. Some pharmacists working in industry allow their licenses to expire because they have no plans to enter active pharmacy practice.

Pharmacy graduates with entry degrees (baccalaureate in pharmacy or Pharm.D.) are actively recruited by the pharmaceutical industry to fill jobs from research to marketing and all of the in-between areas involving quality control, pharmaceutics, pharmaceutical chemistry, writing, public relations, library research, and sales. Pharmacy graduates who continue their studies in graduate schools and earn master of science and/or doctor of philosophy degrees will be placed in industrial positions of greater responsibility and subsequently earn greater incomes commensurate with qualifications.

Industrial Internships for Students

In 1973 seventeen American pharmaceutical manufacturers invited pharmacy students to spend their summer as industrial interns by rotating through various departments of their facilities over an eight-to-ten-week period. This unique program was such a success that by the summer of 1997 approximately twenty-four hundred students had enjoyed this once-in-a-lifetime experience and additional manufacturers were supporting the program.

The American Pharmaceutical Association (APhA) and its Academy of Students of Pharmacy (ASP) now administer the Pharmaceutical Industry Internship Program. The summer internship program lasts for about ten to twelve weeks, and specific timeta-

bles are determined by individual companies, which not only pay interns but reimburse participating students for transportation costs to and from internship sites located across the country. Some companies provide assistance for housing as well. During the summer, students may rotate through departments of research and development, production, quality control, medical information, marketing, and other varied areas of interest.

To qualify for an internship, a student must be in good academic standing in an accredited school of pharmacy and a member of the APhA-ASP. Men and women with one year to complete prior to graduation are given preference by company preceptors. Applications are available in early fall from the deans' offices in all pharmacy schools or from APhA-ASP faculty advisors. A completed application package must be submitted before November 30 of each year to: AphA-ASP, Industry Internship Program, 2215 Constitution Avenue NW, Washington D.C. 20037. An informative brochure may be obtained by writing to the same address. You can also contact APhA online at aphanet.org.

Drug Research and Development

Nonchalant patients routinely take lifesaving drugs with no idea of the huge expenditures of scientific manpower and laboratory resources, dedication, and dollars poured into each prescription vial. In an average year, the pharmaceutical industry screens thousands of chemicals as possible drugs, of which one thousand prove worthy of intense investigation. Years later, perhaps sixteen to twenty compounds may make it to the patient's prescription vial. Research and development of one successful new drug costs a manufacturer an estimated $359 million and usually requires years of concerted

effort on the part of many scientists and technicians. The challenge, excitement, and satisfaction associated with industry continue to lure pharmacy graduates to gainful employment in areas compatible with their interests and ambitions.

The research and development of a drug requires the contributions of many scientists including the organic chemist, biochemist, microbiologist, physiologist, pharmacologist, toxicologist, pathologist, pharmaceutical chemist, and physician. Various teams of personnel will be involved in different companies, but the procedure is similar. A compound begins its journey toward the prescription vial when it is synthesized in the laboratory of the chemist. Organic chemists, biochemists, and pharmaceutical chemists use sophisticated technical procedures to isolate and analyze chemicals before sending them to the biological testing laboratory.

Basic biological testing of a chemical is performed in various animal systems over a period of three to five years. During this time, data are accumulated on the chemical's toxicity, carcinogenicity, and pharmacologic activity. If basic biological testing in animals indicates safety and desired drug action, then everything known about the chemical is compiled and the documentation is forwarded to the Food and Drug Administration. This "investigational new drug" (IND) can then legally be used for clinical evaluation (testing in humans). In preparation for investigative testing in humans, the pharmaceutical chemist begins formulation of the chemical into a human dosage form of tablets, capsules, suspensions, or injectables, depending on the nature of the drug in question.

Meticulous clinical testing of a new drug begins with normal, healthy volunteers to determine the drug's most effective dosage strength, its exact use, and human tolerance of it. The next step is limited clinical studies of the drug in patients suffering from the

disease for which the drug is intended. Success with limited numbers merits widening the investigation to thousands of patients. Data attesting to effectiveness and safety are thereby gathered and submitted to the FDA for approval. Once approval is received, the new drug is further tested and observed for unexpected side reactions or additional positive qualities that may be advertised.

Once the drug's research and development phase has been successfully culminated, the new substance enters quantity production. The active ingredient that has been researched and developed as a recognized therapeutic agent must now be manufactured in large quantities. Additional substances, such as coloring and flavoring agents, inert fillers, stabilizers, preservatives, and other additives may be introduced to arrive at effective dosage forms that can be conveniently taken by patients. Production of the dosage form involves quality control, packaging, labeling, inspecting, storing, and shipping, with constant checking at every stage of production. This highly technical manufacturing stage requires the contributions of many specialists including pharmacists, chemists, engineers, biologists, statisticians, and computer scientists.

Promotion and Marketing of Drugs

The final major undertaking, following years of arduous research, development, and production of a product, is the promotion and marketing of the prescription drug. The manufacturer now announces its new therapeutic agent, reveals its actions and dosage, answers questions about its use, and distributes the drug for dispensing to patients. This complex information campaign is strategically coordinated by a multitude of company personnel including pharmacists, physicians, information specialists, economists, artists,

copywriters, editors, advertisers, market researchers, audiovisual experts, sales representatives, and executive directors.

New nonprescription (over-the-counter) drugs may be brought quickly to the attention of the public by mass media advertising, but complex drugs available by prescription only (legend drugs) must be introduced to health professionals by other means. Precise information about new prescription drugs is transmitted to health professionals through advertisements in professional journals and direct mailings of announcements. Printed materials, videos, slide presentations, and tape recordings are prepared for distribution and exhibition at medical conventions and meetings. Busy physicians, dentists, pharmacists, veterinarians, and other medical specialists are the decision makers whom pharmaceutical manufacturers must reach to ensure recognition of legend drugs. Busy health professionals do not always scan journal or mail advertisements. Manufacturers know the best way to inform the medical world of a new prescription is by person-to-person contacts between health professionals and pharmaceutical sales representatives. But as you will soon read, drug makers are also utilizing direct advertising to the public about prescription drugs.

Pharmaceutical Sales Representatives

Pharmaceutical sales representatives (PSRs) are men and women who act as communication links between companies that produce drugs and professionals who prescribe and dispense them. They are sometimes called *detail* men and women because their major responsibility is to provide all details about their company's drugs when face-to-face with health professionals. Some companies refer to this special personnel category as professional or medical service representatives and others simply as sales representatives. The use

of multiple titles among different manufacturers implies that individuals in this important job seek major and inseparable objectives. The first objective of the representative is to inform the physician of the company's products and answer the physician's questions. The second objective is to increase the company's sales of the drug. If the representative impresses physicians with the merits of the drug, physicians will prescribe it for their patients, and the sales objective will be achieved. Thus both objectives are intertwined, and one cannot be realized without the other.

Pharmacy graduates are highly qualified to serve as PSRs, but to succeed they must possess selling skills and the ability to communicate product information to physicians with clarity and precision. Companies hire sales representatives with college degrees in business, education, liberal arts, and sciences. The pharmacist is familiar with drugs and has this obvious advantage over degree holders in other disciplines competing for positions as representatives.

Companies go to great lengths to prepare sales personnel as representatives for their products. All new representatives undergo a minimum of one month of concentrated training. The training consists of seminars in communication and sales techniques, self-instruction programs with texts and audiotapes, observation field study by accompanying seasoned PSRs in their territories, and testing and evaluation to guarantee acceptable standards of excellence. Representatives must be thoroughly familiar with all of their company's products and knowledgeable about the products of major competitors. The first orientation received by sales representatives is the beginning of an ongoing educational program; a steady flow of information continues to be assimilated for persuasive presentation to health professionals.

Pharmaceutical sales representatives call on physicians, dentists, pharmacists, veterinarians, hospital staffs, other medical specialists,

and pharmacy school personnel. The geographic territory of a representative may include 250 physicians, some of whom must be visited five or more times a year. As the representative must also visit pharmacies, clinics, nursing homes, wholesalers, and hospitals, it is clear that his or her schedule is full and requires considerable travel. Companies usually provide automobiles for this purpose and set mileage rates for compensation.

The typical visit to a physician's office lasts between five and ten minutes and requires planning and alacrity on the part of the PSR. The efforts of the representatives are measured by the sales of prescription products generated in their territories. Physicians welcome PSRs because they consider such visits opportunities to tune in to new developments and gain information that can be valuable to the care of patients. The sales representative gains satisfaction in this vital role of health information specialist. The sales representative disseminates technical information about progress in therapeutics directly related to the welfare of patients.

Pharmaceutical sales representatives have stimulating careers that merge sales acumen with significant contributions to improvement in health care. Median earnings for PSRs in their first year of employment average $56,000. The extroverted pharmacist who can accept this leadership position with enthusiasm and dedication will find the door open for promotions to district sales manager, regional sales director, and other executive roles that, in turn, can lead to a position as an officer within the company.

Consumers Urged to "Ask Your Doctor"

Pharmaceutical makers also appeal directly to consumers for recognition of some of their "prescription only" drugs. Manufacturers of prescription drugs advertise the trade names of their products in

full-page newspaper ads and in television commercials that encourage the public to "ask your doctor" about highly promoted prescription products. In this manner, millions of Americans are reached with medical information formerly reserved for direct and exclusive communication with physicians by trained sales representatives.

Television commercials encourage viewers to call toll-free numbers for additional information and discount coupons (to be presented to a pharmacist along with a doctor's prescription) or to visit the manufacturer's website. Manufacturers also urge patients to ask physicians for trial dosages of the drug in question. Drug makers realize that consumers are more knowledgeable and sophisticated than ever before when it comes to exchanging information and openly discussing their drug regimens with one another. Older Americans talk more about medications than they do about the weather! No longer is there a mystery about prescriptions written in Latin for the purpose of keeping patients in the dark. Consumers are used to the advertising of over-the-counter products and now assimilate information regarding prescription drugs with relative ease.

Industrial Career Benefits

In addition to excellent salaries, industrial careers provide many benefits to employees. Companies offer outstanding pension programs, major medical and life insurance policies, stock investment plans, paid vacations, and sick leave. Industrial employees have five-day workweeks and rarely report for weekend assignments. Dietitians manage company cafeterias and provide employees with breakfasts and lunches at nonprofit prices. Many companies provide convenient transportation for employees, and for those who

drive, there is often free parking. Companies also employ house physicians and sponsor physical health programs and cultural activities for the health and recreation of staff members. And many companies gladly pay tuition costs for employees who attend local universities in the evening to expand their knowledge in special disciplines.

Salaries vary depending upon the qualifications of employees. The median annual salary in 2001 for a scientist with a Ph.D. in pharmacy was approximately $84,000; a baccalaureate in pharmacy may command a starting salary of $51,500 (U.S. Bureau of Labor Statistics). Companies compete for outstanding personnel, and the scarcity of specialized personnel is reflected in the excellence of their incomes. Pharmacists with professional and/or graduate degrees have found lifetime careers in many industrial areas: research and development, pharmaceutical journalism, sales, library information services, legislation lobbying, copyright and patent procedures, production and quality control, marketing, and administration. The pharmaceutical manufacturer looks at employees as members of a large, cooperative family and treats them with fairness and respect. It is unusual to find a disgruntled employee associated with the pharmaceutical industry.

Industry Locations

Pharmaceutical manufacturers are largely concentrated in the thirteen states of California, Connecticut, Delaware, Illinois, Indiana, Michigan, Missouri, New Jersey, New York, North Carolina, Ohio, Pennsylvania, and Virginia. However, sales divisions, distribution facilities, and subsidiary plants of major companies are located throughout the United States, Puerto Rico, and most foreign coun-

tries. Opportunities for overseas assignments are limited, but those with backgrounds in international business, foreign language skills, and domestic experience may gain corporate staff positions within international divisions.

Pharmaceutical Industry Outlook

The outlook for employment in industry is good. The pharmaceutical industry will continue to expand and prosper because it has achieved a position of world leadership with its significant contributions to human health. Bright young men and women will always be needed and recruited to share the drug industry's noble commitment to human longevity and eradication of disease.

10

ACADEMIC CAREERS IN PHARMACY

EDUCATORS IN PHARMACY enjoy the same personal and professional satisfactions that their scholarly counterparts in other professions do. Among these are the knowledge that they are passing on information vital to the good health of humans to an eager, future generation of pharmacists; a kinship with other medical professionals and researchers; and a fulfilling relationship with the students whose futures they impact. All this begins in the college of pharmacy.

Colleges of Pharmacy

Every year thousands of students enter the world of pharmacy by gaining admission to accredited colleges of pharmacy. As the first pharmacy lecture unfolds, everyone begins the journey toward a

vocational destination that materializes with the passage of time and fruition of goals. It is unlikely that new students launch their educations aspiring to emulate the professors and deans of pharmacy who greet them in their first days. Fortunately, though unknown to them at that time, among the freshmen sit the deans and professors who will welcome the students of the future.

Academicians in pharmacy are acknowledged scholars dedicated to implementing an environment of learning in which students may master the knowledge and acquire the skills needed in pharmacy practice. In 2001, according to statistics from the American Association of Colleges of Pharmacy, there were approximately 3,777 full-time and 776 part-time faculty members associated with eighty-three schools of pharmacy in the United States. Amazingly, eighty-three deans of pharmacy and their combined faculties of approximately 4,553 educators provide the pharmacy services required by 270 million people living in the United States! This is a momentous achievement that is often overlooked, despite its far-reaching importance.

The contribution of schools of pharmacy to the economy is immense. The 217,000 pharmacists educated in the United States participate in community pharmacy, health-system pharmacy, hospital pharmacy, industry, administration, government services, sales, education, journalism, and research. Total domestic and overseas sales of drugs produced by American manufacturers now exceed $82 billion annually, and the talent required for this vast array of enterprises has its origin in schools of pharmacy. Each year educators tend to thirty-six thousand professional-degree students (Pharm.D.) and three thousand graduate students (M.S. and Ph.D.) preparing for one of many careers in the spectrum of pharmacy. Graduates of pharmacy schools provide membership fees to organizations that could not exist without such support. Pharma-

cists have journals, magazines, newsletters, and books by the thousands available to them. No wonder it is impossible to estimate the vast impact of pharmacy education upon the nation's economy, let alone its influence on the nation's health and welfare.

Academic Credentials

Men and women joining college faculties often spend eight or more years preparing for their duties as faculty members. Academic qualifications for teaching begin with the entry degree for pharmacy practice and end with the completion of an advanced degree in a chosen discipline. Pharmacy graduates wishing to pursue careers in pharmacy education may then enter graduate schools to complete master of science and/or doctor of philosophy degrees. The master of science degree may require a study program of two years. Candidates for doctor of philosophy degrees usually spend no less than three years of full-time study completing degree requirements, assuming that the master's degree has been previously earned. See Chapter 6 for a general survey of graduate study in pharmaceutical sciences.

Academic credentials beyond a pharmacy entry degree are usually essential for careers in education, but there is no hard and fast rule on this. Although the majority of pharmacy professors earned entry pharmacy degrees prior to additional study, faculty specialists in microbiology, physiology, pharmacology, and medicinal chemistry may be nonpharmacy scholars holding advanced degrees in biology or chemistry. Most key faculty members in schools of pharmacy have a Ph.D. The title of doctor does not necessarily indicate an individual's capabilities as an educator, but the prevalence of the Ph.D. credential among pharmacy educators is not to be denied. Teaching rosters of pharmacy schools also include indi-

viduals with M.S. and Pharm.D. degrees as well as master of public health, doctor of veterinary medicine, and other relevant degrees.

Activities of Academicians

Academic careers in pharmacy encompass four main activities: teaching, scholarship and research, administrative services, and student inculcation of values. All four spheres of responsibility are multifaceted and challenging to educators. The faculty member who participates in all four activities is an all-around educator. There are all-around educators in pharmacy; but there are also those who choose to concentrate on research, others who must devote total energy to administration, and those with schedules that limit their activities to teaching. The fourth activity (student inculcation of values) is most difficult to define and not always acknowledged by academics because of its intangible qualities. Abstracts of the four main activities of academics will shed some light on what it is like to be a professor in a school of pharmacy.

Teaching in a School of Pharmacy

There are many aspects to teaching in a school of pharmacy. Areas in which professors majored as graduate students are the ones that occupy their teaching time. Faculty members teach undergraduate students, graduate students, and alumni returning for continuing education courses. Holding an advanced degree is a vital prerequisite for the professor who provides instruction to graduate students working toward master of science and/or doctor of philosophy degrees.

Classes may be conducted in a lecture hall that seats one hundred undergraduate students or in a conference room with ten or

fewer graduate students. Continuing education courses may be offered in the evening or on a weekend afternoon when alumni are free to attend. Teachers may be assigned to summer session instruction. Instruction may also occur one-on-one in supervised laboratory exercises or in areas outside the school, such as clinics or departments of a health sciences center. No matter what the size of the class or the nature of the student, a good teacher has command of the subject, is familiar with advances in the field, organizes material with care, presents it with force and clarity, relates the subject to other fields, and stimulates learning.

Teaching does not end with the delivery of a lecture. Faculty members tutor students requiring special assistance and offer guidance for the improvement of study habits. The final act of teaching involves the submission of grades for students. Grades are usually determined through the teacher's examinations, which are reliable tools of evaluation. Many universities consider the normal teaching load to be twelve lecture hours per week, which involves many additional hours of library work and preparation of polished lectures. Full-time lecturing may not allow teachers sufficient additional time for research activities.

Faculty Members and Research

Scholarship and research activities of faculty members entail investigations to discover or revise facts, theories, and applications of knowledge. The purpose of original research is to enlighten and to improve the quality of life. Researchers in pharmacy may be concerned with the synthesis of new drugs, evaluation of new uses for old drugs, patterns of patient-pharmacist relations, or the investigation of absorption and excretion rates of drugs from the body. There is no limit to the type of research that may be conducted in a school of pharmacy.

Professors conduct independent research or join graduate students in cooperative research efforts that lead to publication of articles in scholarly and professional journals. A professor, who acts as a student's mentor by offering guidance and encouragement, directs the thesis of the graduate student. Research efforts are reflected by frequency of publication on the part of faculty members, although the quality of productivity is more important than the quantity. The professor who publishes research results in four segments may have representation in four issues of a journal, but, in the long run, the quality of the research will determine its significance.

To obtain nonuniversity research funding, professors submit written outlines of proposed projects to funding agencies. If approved, these proposals could result in grants valued at thousands of dollars. The funding of research projects by government and private sources are additional indications of a professor's recognition as a researcher. Some studies indicate that 10 percent of U.S. academics publish about 90 percent of journal articles. It has been written that researchers must possess creative tension, innate talent, acquired skills, drive, and competitiveness to succeed. Teachers may demonstrate scholarship by writing textbooks, book reviews, reports, and articles not necessarily consisting of original research. Those deep in research may have to limit their teaching schedules, just as faculty members carrying full teaching loads may not have sufficient time to engage in research.

Administration and Education

Administrative services involve managing transactions or operations. Faculty members' involvement in administrative matters

depends on their academic rank and assigned responsibilities in the hierarchy of the college. In a school of pharmacy, the burden of administration rests with the dean, who is ultimately accountable for the successes and failures of the institution. Deans are involved with budget management, policy making, personnel selection, alumni relations, student admissions, report making, and other administrative duties. As the principal representative of a school, the dean serves as delegate to countless conventions, meetings, and banquets, necessitating the capacity to listen well, stay awake, and digest predictable platters of baked, broiled, fried, and fricasseed chicken dinners.

Deans require assistance in performing their roles and often appoint associate and/or assistant deans to share the administrative load. Faculty members serve as chairpersons of departments made up of colleagues in the same discipline. A school of pharmacy may have departments of social/administrative sciences, pharmaceutics, pharmaceutical chemistry, pharmacy practice, and pharmacology. These departments meet periodically, and chairpersons serve as departmental liaisons to the dean. Most schools have assemblies where faculty members serve as officers and committee members. Professors act administratively by recruiting students, serving on civic committees, coordinating job placement of students, advising extracurricular groups, providing references for graduates, and participating on faculty committees that revise curricula, admit applicants, and deal with grievances. Administrative responsibilities of faculty members vary from school to school, but there are management assignments in most institutions. Deans are so overwhelmed with administrative assignments that few find time to teach or engage in research. However, men and women

appointed to deanships have been accorded the honor in recognition of prior outstanding teaching, scholarship, and administrative accomplishments.

Professors and Student Character Development

Although both good and great teachers are adept at teaching pharmacy, the difference between them is that the great teacher also encourages self-realization and individual development of students. Pharmacy professors tell their students to "do more than just fill prescriptions" when serving patients, but teachers sometimes limit their relationships with students to disclosure of information. Specialists in education have noted that students almost universally link their most profound educational experiences to teachers with whom they have had some personal relationship in and out of the classroom.

Individual development of students is aided by treating them as promising equals, expressing faith in their abilities, and providing suitable prototypes in adult society. Teachers who aim for the fullest possible development of students take a personal interest in them through empathic communication. Faculty members who relate to students with enthusiasm and combine character-developing and informational functions enjoy roles as advisors to pharmacy fraternities, honor societies, professional associations, and student governments. The clock is the archenemy of this aspect of academic careers in pharmacy. Faculty members must meet responsibilities of teaching, tutoring, researching, writing, and administration. All in all, pharmacy education has met the challenge of full development among students because many exceptional men and women have emerged from schools of pharmacy to accept leadership posi-

tions and better society through decision making, criticism, and creative activity.

Academic Recognition

Most occupations rank participants according to achievement, experience, and qualifications. The U.S. Army grades soldiers from privates to generals, but few privates gain the rank of general! In hospital pharmacy the fledgling pharmacist begins as a staff pharmacist with hopes for gradual promotion to assistant director, associate director, and, finally, chief pharmacist within the same hospital or a similarly advanced position in another hospital. In an academic career, a teacher may begin as an instructor and be promoted to assistant professor, associate professor, and professor.

Instructors usually hold master of science degrees and are simultaneously working toward doctor of philosophy degrees. Promotion to assistant professor may be based on the instructor's attainment of the doctor's degree or upon experience as a teacher and scholarly promise. Promotion from assistant to associate professor may be based on continued growth as a teacher and scholar or capacity for independent research. For promotion from associate to full professor, the candidate must achieve professional recognition and contribute significant academic, administrative, and professional services to the institution.

Procedures for promotion vary from one school to another but usually involve departmental and peer evaluation with final recommendation from the dean. A faculty member's teaching, research, scholarship, and administrative services can be assessed to some extent by counting hours of instruction and number of

students, publications and grants received, books and articles published, and hours spent in committee meetings and management activities. Inculcation of values and character development of students are impossible to measure and are largely ignored as criteria for promotion.

Rewards of Academia

Faculty members of schools of pharmacy enjoy numerous employee benefits including pension programs; life, health, and disability insurance; tax-sheltered annuities; free or reduced college tuition for family; discounts for school athletic events, theatricals, and bookstore purchases; and a tenure policy. The tenure policy ensures faculty members employment for life or until the age of retirement is reached. Tenure is usually granted to associate and full professors after three or more years and to assistant professors who have held office for six or more years. Under specified conditions, faculty members may apply for study leaves of one or two semesters for scholarly pursuit and receive full salary for a one-semester leave or half salary for a two-semester leave. Faculty benefits vary from school to school but, because of the unifying influence of the American Association of University Professors (1012 Fourteenth Street NW, Suite 500, Washington, D.C. 20005, aaup.org) and the emergence of a major national retirement program in a majority of schools, differences are slight. Schools of pharmacy are located in all states except Alaska, Delaware, Hawaii, Maine, Nevada, New Hampshire, and Vermont. There are schools of pharmacy in metropolitan cities, small towns, and rural areas. Educators have varied climates and environments to select from in choosing the institution that may serve as an employment base for many years.

Teachers are salaried on the basis of calendar year (twelve-month) or academic year (ten-month) appointments. The 2002–03 faculty salary survey of the American Association of Colleges of Pharmacy (AACP) gathered income statistics from all schools of pharmacy encompassing more than thirty-one hundred full-time faculty members in pharmacy-related disciplines. Calendar-year salaries averaged as follows:

Pharmacy deans	$159,407
Professors	$104,469
Associate professors	$81,925
Assistant professors	$71,629
Instructors	$63,477

There is ample evidence that pharmacy educators are meeting their objectives through dynamic curricula that provide the education, training, and experiences necessary for graduates to gain professional competence. The thrill of being an educator comes from the awareness that your contributions are embodied in the achievements of graduates. It is satisfying to learn that former students are owners of community pharmacies or executives with drug manufacturers. It is exciting to learn that former students have joined hospital practice or been promoted to professors and deanships in pharmacy schools. There will always be faculty positions available for qualified men and women who wish to perpetuate the traditions of pharmaceutical education.

11

Public Pharmacy Practice

Public pharmacists are pharmacists employed by federal, state, and city agencies and compensated with governmental revenues. The paths pharmacists in public service can take are diverse and offer limitless opportunities for fulfillment.

United States Public Health Service

The United States Public Health Service (PHS), a major component of the Department of Health and Human Services, is one of the largest health services in the world. The PHS safeguards the nation's health through eight operating divisions:

1. Agency for Health Care Policy and Research
2. Agency for Toxic Substances and Disease Registry
3. Centers for Disease Control and Prevention
4. Food and Drug Administration
5. Health Resources and Services Administration

6. Indian Health Service
7. National Institutes of Health
8. Substance Abuse and Mental Health Services Administration

The Public Health Service also provides professionals for other federal programs such as the Bureau of Prisons, Health Care Financing Administration, Immigration and Naturalization Service, Coast Guard, Environmental Protection Agency, District of Columbia's Commission on Mental Health Services, and for international assignments.

Pharmacists working for the PHS may be employed as civilians (Civil Service) or as uniformed health professionals (Commissioned Corps). In 2002 the Commissioned Corps of the PHS consisted of approximately six thousand health professionals, including about 1,600 physicians, 1,000 nurses, and 760 pharmacists, in addition to dentists, veterinarians, dietitians, sanitarians, and other scientists. As Rear Admiral Fred G. Paavola, former Chief Pharmacist for the Public Health Service, noted: "The PHS provides pharmacists with exciting practice opportunities including working directly from the patient's medical record as the basis for providing pharmaceutical care, participating in the development and implementation of a research protocol for a new drug, or reviewing clinical data as part of the approval process of a new drug product. Pharmacists also provide leadership for program development and health policy throughout PHS and other federal programs."

Pharmacists holding entry degrees (baccalaureate in pharmacy or doctor of pharmacy) or graduate degrees (M.S. or Ph.D.) are eligible for appointment to the Commissioned Corps of the PHS. Applicants must be younger than forty-four years of age, United States citizens, and must meet medical health requirements. Unlike

Civil Service counterparts, officers in the corps are subject to assignment wherever they are needed. Corps benefits are similar to those for officers in the military, including board-certified pay, quarters allowance, subsistence allowance, noncontributory retirement, medical care of dependents, annual leave of thirty calendar days, and fulfillment of selective service obligations (after two years of service). All initial appointments are to the Reserve Corps on three-year probationary periods. Maximum retirement pay is obtained after thirty years of service, based on 75 percent times the average of the highest three years of base pay. For information and application, pharmacists may contact:

> Recruitment Branch
> Commissioned Corps, PHS
> Parklawn Building
> 5600 Fishers Lane
> Rockville, Maryland 20857
> (800) 279-1605
> dhhs.gov

Indian Health Service

The Indian Health Service (IHS) provides a comprehensive, broad-based, community-oriented health delivery system to more than 1.5 million American Indians and Alaskan Natives who are members of approximately 550 federally recognized tribes. The health delivery system includes hospital and ambulatory medical care, prevention and rehabilitation services, and development of community sanitation facilities.

Approximately 540 pharmacists, assisted by technicians, are responsible for diagnosing and treating outpatients with certain

acute diseases, managing conditions of outpatients with certain chronic diseases, and exercising independent judgment for the care of such patients in 49 hospitals, 180 health centers, 106 health stations, 8 school health centers, 167 Alaskan village clinics, and 34 urban projects consisting of health clinics and community service facilities. Indian Health Service pharmacists carry out primary care responsibilities by obtaining the patient's history, taking vital signs, requesting lab tests, performing physical diagnostic techniques, evaluating data, and determining a treatment plan according to established IHS treatment protocols. For further information contact:

Indian Health Service
5600 Fishers Lane
Rockville, Maryland 20857
ihs.gov

Food and Drug Administration

The Food and Drug Administration (FDA) regulates the safety and effectiveness of human and veterinary drugs, biological products, and medical devices, as well as the food and cosmetic industry. The FDA regulates products representing 25 percent of every dollar a consumer spends, and its professional personnel protect the public from unsafe, ineffective, and misleading products.

The FDA employs more than eighty-five hundred scientists nationwide including physicians, pharmacists, nurses, pharmacologists, chemists, microbiologists, engineers, psychologists, and others. Each year these professionals approve hundreds of new and generic drugs for marketing, conduct thousands of inspections, and

oversee product recalls and seizures. The FDA relies on the knowledge, expertise, and dedication of its health personnel, scientists, and engineers in the ongoing protection of the public health.

Pharmacists at the FDA coordinate the review of new and generic drug application information from the regulated industry, including bioavailability and bioequivalency test data; review labeling information; and investigate complaints of injury, illness, or death caused by an FDA-regulated product. Exciting and challenging opportunities exist at the FDA, and qualified individuals work closely with some of the foremost medical, pharmaceutical, and regulatory authorities in the world. Some health professionals only dream about making a difference and improving the lives of people, but health professionals at the FDA make a real difference in the lives of Americans every day. Contact the FDA at:

Food and Drug Administration
5600 Fishers Lane
Rockville, Maryland 20857
(888) 463-6322
fda.gov

Federal Bureau of Prisons

The Federal Bureau of Prisons (BOP) is an agency of the United States Department of Justice, which is a department under the jurisdiction of the Attorney General. Its mission is to protect society by confining offenders in the controlled environments of prisons and community-based facilities that are safe, humane, and appropriately secure, while providing work and other self-improvement opportunities to assist offenders in becoming law-abiding citizens.

The Bureau of Prisons operates one hundred institutions in urban and rural areas in forty states with plans for at least thirty additional facilities by 2006. These institutions include six medical referral centers, such as rehabilitation services, major surgery, and intensive psychiatric care, to meet the special needs of offenders. Eighty-four facilities are ambulatory sites usually staffed by teams of two physicians, two dentists, six to ten mid-level providers, technical and administrative assistants, and a pharmacy unit.

Most of the bureau's 150 pharmacists are involved in direct patient care. Pharmacists fill medication orders directly from patients' charts and have complete access to all medical information. Bureau pharmacists also provide appropriate counseling to patients. Some pharmacists participate in diabetic and hypertensive clinics, infectious disease monitoring, mental health chronic-care clinics, rounds with physicians, and counseling of discharged offenders. Approximately 10 percent of pharmacists have gained administrative roles in the agency, with most functioning as health service administrators.

In 1994 the Bureau of Prisons made the significant commitment to pursue accreditation by the Joint Commission on Accreditation of Health Care Organizations. Approximately 30 percent of facilities have been granted accreditation as of 2002. Pharmacists with the Bureau of Prisons play a major role in the success of the commitment to quality. Contact the BOP at:

Bureau of Prisons
320 First Street NW
Washington, D.C. 20534
(888) 317-8455
bop.gov

United States Coast Guard Pharmacists

The United States Coast Guard is the smallest of the armed services. Its health-care program looks after thirty-six thousand active-duty personnel and their dependents as well as retirees and their dependents. Family-oriented primary health-care programs are available at thirty shore-based Coast Guard clinics of which thirteen are staffed with pharmacy officers of the United States Public Health Service. As a Public Health Service commissioned officer detailed to the Coast Guard, the pharmacist is a military officer of the armed forces and is subject to all applicable laws, regulations, and policies including all provisions of the Uniform Code of Military Justice. Contact the Medical Recruitment Office at (800) 800-2676 for general information and application procedures.

Veterans Affairs Pharmacy Service

The Veterans Health Services and Research Administration offers numerous employment opportunities for civilian pharmacists in medical centers, clinics, and nursing care units. (The VA is separate and apart from the United States Public Health Service.) A Veterans Affairs publication recently announced that it "offers pharmacists a challenging and varied program in areas of pharmacy administration, clinical pharmacy, inpatient and outpatient dispensing, medication systems, bulk compounding and formula development, and research in professional and administrative problems."

There are 4,371 licensed public pharmacists practicing in medical centers, nursing home care units, and outpatient clinics of the Department of Veterans Affairs (U.S. Office of Personnel Management). For entry positions, applicants must hold at least a five-

year pharmacy degree from an accredited school, have completed at least a one-year clerkship or internship, and be licensed in a state or territory of the United States or the District of Columbia.

Initial appointment into the Veterans Pharmacy Service is at grade GS-9, which in 2000 paid public pharmacists a minimum salary of $32,380 and a maximum of $42,091. Most grade GS-9 pharmacists are newly graduated men and women. Additional education, training, or experience is required for grades GS-11 and above. Most staff pharmacists are ranked grade GS-11, with annual incomes ranging from $39,178 to $50,932. Salaries vary with geographical placements so as to compete with the incomes of nongovernment pharmacists. Supervisory pharmacists may earn up to $63,281, assistant pharmacy chiefs up to $76,978, and chief pharmacists up to $85,774. VA pharmacists may be promoted to grade GS-14 (chief pharmacist). A recent VA publication revealed that over 80 percent of VA pharmacists are in grades GS-11 through GS-14 (U.S. Office of Personnel Management, General Schedule).

There is now general agreement that the VA must gain cost-consciousness in the administration of its $17 billion annual budget, the operation of the nation's largest hospital system, and the servicing of ten million veterans. In the 1990s the VA eliminated seventeen thousand jobs along with nine thousand beds in VA hospitals nationwide. The VA anticipates that 65 percent of procedures performed at its hospitals will be on an outpatient basis rather than the inpatient treatment so long identified with VA practices.

The Veterans Administration was established in 1930 to administer federally funded programs providing benefits to America's veterans. Over the years it has fulfilled this responsibility through a nationwide network of health-care centers, benefits offices, counseling centers, data processing centers, and national cemeteries. Pub-

lic pharmacists play an important role in this agency's health-care delivery services, and they enjoy significant benefits available to the federal government's civilian workhorse. Contact the VA at:

Department of Veterans Affairs
810 Vermont Avenue NW
Washington, D.C. 20420
(202) 273-4800
va.gov

Civil Service Commission Pharmacists

Civil Service Commission pharmacists are not under the auspices of the United States Public Health Service nor are they paid directly by the federal government. Civil Service pharmacists are hired by state, county, or city agencies located within the confines of a particular state in the United States. Examples cited for the Commonwealth of Pennsylvania serve as a blueprint for hiring policies within other states in America.

Pennsylvania requires that pharmacists seeking employment under its Civil Service Commission be residents of Pennsylvania, possess a license issued by the Pennsylvania State Board of Pharmacy, be capable of performing essential functions of the job, and possess good moral character. Veterans of the armed forces and widows and widowers of veterans are extended preference for Civil Service positions. Students who are enrolled in Pennsylvania pharmacy schools and who have Pennsylvania mailing addresses, even though they are out-of-state students, are eligible to apply for positions, but following graduation they must demonstrate intent to continue residing in Pennsylvania.

Pharmacists are assigned positions throughout Pennsylvania's sixty-seven counties. The State Department of Public Welfare and the Department of Military Affairs employ fifty-eight pharmacists and twenty-two chief pharmacists. On the average, six new pharmacists and two new chief pharmacists are hired each year, depending on normal turnover due to retirements, promotions, transfers, and resignations. In addition to the previously noted pharmacy positions, six "drug program specialists" are located in regional offices of the Department of State of Pennsylvania. At the time of this writing, one specialist was located in Allegheny County, one in Lackawanna County, and two in Philadelphia County. Vacancies existed in Dauphin and Allegheny Counties. Drug program specialists are pharmacists who perform professional inspections and investigative work in the regulation of pharmacies within the Commonwealth of Pennsylvania.

Armed Forces

The armed forces offer exciting opportunities for pharmacists as commissioned officers in the Air Force, Army, and Navy. Just as the VA provides medical care to men and women honorably discharged from the armed forces, the Department of Defense (defenselink .mil) provides health care to active-duty personnel and their families through the operation of hospitals, minihospitals, and clinics in the United States and abroad. Military pharmacists receive the same basic pay as other officers in the same rank, depending upon time in service. Military pharmacists may retire after twenty years of service with 40 percent of their base pay, and the maximum retirement benefit to pharmacists is 75 percent of base pay following thirty years of service.

A look at one other branch of the armed forces will provide additional insight to pharmacists considering military careers. The Air Force Personnel Center reports that as of 2002 there were 67,719 officers among its ranks, including 227 pharmacist officers. Enlisted Air Force personnel numbered 280,078 including several superintendents or chief manager pharmacists, and more than 1,200 men and women attached to pharmacies of the Air Force across the nation and around the world (U.S. Department of Defense). Air Force pharmacists usually enter the service as either second or first lieutenants, with a starting pay ranging from $39,000 to $55,000 depending on entry grade, marital status, and military service, if any. Salaries increase as years of service grow and ranks rise. Air Force members receive free comprehensive medical and dental care, quarters allowance, access to military commissaries and exchanges (supermarkets and department stores), tax-free benefits, and thirty days vacation annually along with numerous other benefits.

Peace Corps

Since President John F. Kennedy issued an executive order to create the Peace Corps on March 1, 1961, more than 150,000 American volunteers have gone abroad to share their skills and energies with people in the developing world. At the invitation of host governments, dedicated Americans have served in ninety-four countries.

Approximately seven thousand volunteers are now working abroad in 130 countries (*Occupational Outlook Quarterly*, Fall 2000). Volunteers with degrees or certification in health fields are in great demand to work in public health education, to train host country coworkers, and to coordinate community projects dealing with adult education in health care. The diversified education of

pharmacists provides them with a wealth of knowledge, experience, and creativity enabling them to help people help themselves in their fight against hunger, disease, poverty, and lack of opportunity.

Most Peace Corps assignments are for two years and begin after successful completion of training sessions lasting eight to fourteen weeks that are usually held in host countries. A living allowance in the local currency covers housing, food, full health benefits, and other essentials, and includes a little spending money. Upon completion of service, volunteers receive a readjustment allowance (currently $225) for every month served in the Peace Corps. Vacation time is accrued at two days per month, and participants are encouraged to use their vacation time to travel in the host country.

Why would any pharmacist volunteer to serve two years as a member of the Peace Corps? The benefits of Peace Corps affiliation are personal enrichment, satisfaction, and fulfillment plus the chance to learn about one's strengths and weaknesses in ways that would not be possible at home. Peace Corps people want to help others. They want to improve the lives of others; they want to impart their knowledge and skills; they want to make the world a better place; and they want to be catalysts of change.

Career benefits include language and skills training, hands-on experience in the developing world, and unusual educational opportunities. For those who qualify, repayment of Federal Perkins Loans are substantially reduced and the interest on these loans canceled for a full two years of Peace Corps service. More than fifty graduate schools provide scholarships for returning volunteers, and some universities offer limited academic credit for Peace Corps service. People who invest a few years of their lives for the unselfish purpose of helping the less fortunate are very special human beings, and they are rewarded with the intangibles that are reflected upon for a lifetime. There is no doubt that future employers will be

impressed with the inclusion of Peace Corps service on a résumé! There are eleven Peace Corps recruitment offices throughout the United States. Additional information about Peace Corps service may be obtained by calling (800) 424-8580 or logging on to peacecorps.gov.

A Growing Specialty: Public Pharmacy

The avenues of public pharmacy practice run in countless directions. Pharmacy practitioners do well to be inquisitive about opportunities in public pharmacy. The benefits, challenges, adventures, travel, professionalism, and stimulation of public pharmacy deserve more attention and consideration on the part of young graduates.

It is not possible to present all of the openings that exist for pharmacists in government service. New positions appear every year as the needs of federal, state, county, and city governments fluctuate with a changing society. Men and women with entry degrees in pharmacy and those with graduate degrees in pharmaceutical sciences have gained association with the Agency for Toxic Substances and Disease Registry, National Institute on Drug Abuse, National Institute of Mental Health, National Institute on Alcohol Abuse and Alcoholism, Centers for Disease Control, National Institutes of Health, Environmental Protection Agency, and the Drug Enforcement Administration.

Unusual opportunities exist for pharmacists working with governmental agencies at all levels. Public pharmacy is a fast-growing specialty of pharmacy practice. Don't overlook this career option.

Appendix A

National Pharmacy Associations

American Association of Colleges of Pharmacy
1426 Prince St.
Alexandria, VA 22314
aacp.org

American Association of Pharmaceutical Sciences
2107 Wilson Blvd., Ste. 700
Arlington, VA 22201
aaps.org

American Association of Pharmacy Technicians
P.O. Box 1447
Greensboro, NC 27402
pharmacytechnician.com

American Council on Pharmaceutical Education
20 N. Clark St., Ste. 2500
Chicago, IL 60602
acpe.org

American Foundation for Pharmaceutical Education
One Church St., Ste. 2
Rockville, MD 20850
afpenet.org

American Pharmaceutical Association
2215 Constitution Ave. NW
Washington, DC 20037-2985
aphanet.org

American Public Health Association
800 I St. NW
Washington, DC 20001
apha.org

American Society of Consultant Pharmacists
1321 Duke St.
Alexandria, VA 22314
ascp.com

American Society of Health-System Pharmacists
7272 Wisconsin Ave.
Bethesda, MD 20814
ashp.org

Drug Information Association
501 Office Center Dr., Ste. 450
Fort Washington, PA 19034
diahome.org

National Association of Boards of Pharmacy
700 Busse Highway
Park Ridge, IL 60068
nabp.net

National Association of Chain Drug Stores
413 N. Lee St.
P.O. Box 1417-D49
Alexandria, VA 22313-1480
nacds.org

National Community Pharmacists Association
205 Daingerfield Rd.
Alexandria, VA 22314
ncpanet.org

National Council for Prescription Drug Programs
9240 E. Raintree Dr.
Scottsdale, AZ 85260
ncpdp.org

Pharmaceutical Research and Manufacturers of America
1100 Fifteenth St. NW
Washington, DC 20005
phrma.org

U.S. Pharmacopeia
12601 Twinbrook Pkwy.
Rockville, MD 20852
usp.org

Appendix B

Selected Periodicals

America's Pharmacist
National Community Pharmacists Association
205 Daingerfield Rd.
Alexandria, VA 22314

American Journal of Health-System Pharmacists
American Society of Health-System Pharmacists
7272 Wisconsin Ave.
Bethesda, MD 20814

American Journal of Pharmaceutical Education
American Association of Colleges of Pharmacy
1426 Prince St.
Alexandria, VA 22314

American Journal of Public Health
800 I St. NW
Washington, DC 20001

Annals of Pharmacotherapy
8044 Montgomery Rd., Ste. 415
Cincinnati, OH 45236-2919

Clinical Consultant
American Society of Consultant Pharmacists
1321 Duke St.
Alexandria, VA 22314

Clinical Pharmacology and Therapeutics
American Society for Pharmacology and Experimental Therapeutics
528 N. Washington St.
Alexandria, VA 22314

Drug Topics
Medical Economics Co., Inc.
Five Paragon Dr.
Montvale, NJ 07645

Journal of the American Pharmaceutical Association
American Pharmaceutical Association
2215 Constitution Ave. NW
Washington, DC 20037-2985

Journal of Pharmaceutical Sciences
John Wiley & Sons, Inc.
605 Third Ave.
New York, NY 10158

Pharmaceutical Research
American Association of Pharmaceutical Scientists
2107 Wilson Blvd., Ste. 700
Arlington, VA 22201-3046

Pharmacy Times
1065 Old Country Rd., Ste. 213
Westbury, NY 11590

U.S. Pharmacist
Jobson Publishing
100 Avenue of the Americas
New York, NY 10013

Colleges and Schools of Pharmacy Offering Professional Programs

THERE ARE EIGHTY-THREE schools and colleges of pharmacy located in forty-three states, Puerto Rico, and the District of Columbia. There are no pharmacy institutions of higher education in the states of Alaska, Delaware, Hawaii, Maine, Nevada, New Hampshire, and Vermont. (Please note the following key: 1 = Pharm.D., first professional degree; 2 = Pharm.D. as a post–B.S. degree.)

Alabama

Auburn University (1, 2)
School of Pharmacy
217 Pharmacy Building
Auburn, AL 36849-5501
auburn.edu

Samford University (1)
McWhorter School of Pharmacy
800 Lakeshore Dr.
Birmingham, AL 35229
samford.edu

Arizona

Midwestern University (1)
School of Pharmacy
19555 N. Fifty-Ninth Ave.
Glendale, AZ 85308
midwestern.edu

University of Arizona (1)
College of Pharmacy
P.O. Box 210207
Tucson, AZ 85721-0207
arizona.edu

Arkansas

University of Arkansas for Medical Sciences (1, 2)
College of Pharmacy
4301 W. Markham St., Slot 522
Little Rock, AK 72205-7122
uams.edu/cop/default

California

University of California, San Francisco (1)
School of Pharmacy
San Francisco, CA 94143-0446
ucsf.edu

University of the Pacific (1, 2)
Thomas J. Long School of Pharmacy
3601 Pacific Ave.
Stockton, CA 95211
uop.edu

University of Southern California (1, 2)
School of Pharmacy
1985 Zonal Ave.
Los Angeles, CA 90033-1086
usc.edu

Western University of Health Sciences (1)
College of Pharmacy
309 E. Second St.
Pomona, CA 91766-1854
westernu.edu

Colorado

University of Colorado (1)
School of Pharmacy
4200 E. Ninth Ave., C-238
Denver, CO 80262-0238
cudenver.edu

Connecticut

University of Connecticut (1)
School of Pharmacy
P.O. Box U-92, Unit 2092
372 Fairfield Rd.
Storrs, CT 06269-2092
uconn.edu

District of Columbia

Howard University (1, 2)
College of Pharmacy, Nursing, and Allied Health
2300 Fourth St. NW
Washington, DC 20059
howard.edu

Florida

Florida Agricultural and Mechanical University (1, 2)
College of Pharmacy
P.O. Box 367
Tallahassee, FL 32307-3800
famu.edu

Nova Southeastern University (1, 2)
College of Pharmacy
3200 S. University Dr.
Ft. Lauderdale, FL 33328
nova.edu

Palm Beach Atlantic College (1)
School of Pharmacy
901 S. Flagler Dr.
West Palm Beach, FL 33416
pbac.edu

University of Florida (1, 2)
College of Pharmacy Science
Health Science Center
P.O. Box 100484
Gainesville, FL 32610-0484
ufl.edu

Georgia

Mercer University (1, 2)
Southern School of Pharmacy
3001 Mercer University Dr.
Atlanta, GA 30341-4415
mercer.edu

University of Georgia (1, 2)
College of Pharmacy
D.W. Brooks Dr.
Athens, GA 30602-2351
uga.edu

Idaho

Idaho State University (1, 2)
College of Pharmacy
P.O. Box 8288
Pocatello, ID 83209-8288
isu.edu

Illinois

Midwestern University (1, 2)
Chicago College of Pharmacy
555 Thirty-First St.
Downers Grove, IL 60515-1235
midwestern.edu

University of Illinois at Chicago (1, 2)
College of Pharmacy
833 S. Wood St., M/C 874
Chicago, IL 60612-8230
uic.edu

Indiana

Butler University (1)
College of Pharmacy and Health Sciences
4600 Sunset Ave.
Indianapolis, IN 46208
butler.edu

Purdue University (1, 2)
School of Pharmacy and Pharmaceutical Sciences
1330 Heine Pharmacy Building
West Lafayette, IN 47907-1330
purdue.edu

Iowa

Drake University (1, 2)
College of Pharmacy
2507 University Ave.
Des Moines, IA 50311-4505
drake.edu

University of Iowa (1, 2)
College of Pharmacy
Iowa City, IA 52242
uiowa.edu

Kansas

University of Kansas (1, 2)
School of Pharmacy
2056 Malott Hall
Lawrence, KS 66045-2500
ku.edu

Kentucky

University of Kentucky (1, 2)
College of Pharmacy
Rose St.
Lexington, KY 40536-0082
uky.edu

Louisiana

University of Louisiana at Monroe (1)
School of Pharmacy
700 University Ave.
Monroe, LA 71209-0470
ulm.edu

Xavier University of Louisiana (1, 2)
College of Pharmacy
7325 Palmetto St.
New Orleans, LA 70125
xula.edu

Maryland

University of Maryland at Baltimore (1, 2)
School of Pharmacy
20 N. Pine St.
Baltimore, MD 21201-1180
umaryland.edu

Massachusetts

Massachusetts College of Pharmacy and Health Sciences (1, 2)
179 Longwood Ave.
Boston, MA 02115-5896
and (1)
19 Foster St.
Worcester, MA 01608
mcp.edu

Northeastern University (1)
Bouve College of Pharmacy
360 Huntington Ave.
Boston, MA 02115
neu.edu

Michigan

Ferris State University (1)
College of Pharmacy
220 Ferris Dr.
Big Rapids, MI 49307-2740
ferris.edu

University of Michigan (1, 2)
College of Pharmacy
428 Church St.
Ann Arbor, MI 48109-1065
umich.edu

Wayne State University (1, 2)
College of Pharmacy
105 Shapero Hall
Detroit, MI 48202-3489
wayne.edu

Minnesota

University of Minnesota (1, 2)
College of Pharmacy
308 Harvard St. SE
5-130 Weaver-Densford Hall
Minneapolis, MN 55455-0343
umn.edu

Mississippi

University of Mississippi (1, 2)
School of Pharmacy
P.O. Box 1848
University, MS 38677-9814
olemiss.edu

Missouri

St. Louis College of Pharmacy (1, 2)
4588 Parkview Pl.
St. Louis, MO 63110-1088
stlcop.edu

University of Missouri–Kansas City (1, 2)
School of Pharmacy
5005 Rockhill Rd.
Kansas City, MO 64110-2499
umkc.edu

Montana

University of Montana (1, 2)
School of Pharmacy and Allied Health Sciences
32 Campus Dr.
Missoula, MT 59812-1075
umt.edu

Nebraska

Creighton University (1, 2)
School of Pharmacy and Allied Health Professions
2500 California Plaza
Omaha, NE 68178
creighton.edu

University of Nebraska Medical Center (1)
College of Pharmacy
600 S. Forty-Second St.
Omaha, NE 68198-6000
unmc.edu

New Jersey

Rutgers State University of New Jersey (1, 2)
College of Pharmacy
160 Frelinghuysen Rd.
Piscataway, NJ 08855-0789
rutgers.edu

New Mexico

University of New Mexico (1, 2)
College of Pharmacy
Health Sciences Center
Albuquerque, NM 87131-1066
unm.edu

New York

Albany College of Pharmacy (1, 2)
Union University
106 New Scotland Ave.
Albany, NY 12208
acp.edu

Long Island University (1, 2)
Arnold and Marie Schwartz College of Pharmacy
75 DeKalb Ave. at University Plaza
Brooklyn, NY 11201
liu.edu

St. John's University (1, 2)
College of Pharmacy and Allied Health Professions
8000 Utopia Pkwy.
Jamaica, NY 11439
stjohns.edu/pls/portal30/sjudev.school.pharmacy

State University of New York at Buffalo (1, 2)
School of Pharmacy
C 126 Cooke-Hochstetter Complex
Amherst, NY 14260-1200
buffalo.edu

North Carolina

Campbell University (1, 2)
School of Pharmacy
Buies Creek, NC 27506
campbell.edu

University of North Carolina at Chapel Hill (1, 2)
School of Pharmacy
Beard Hall-CB #7360
Chapel Hill, NC 27599-7360
unc.edu

North Dakota

North Dakota State University (1, 2)
College of Pharmacy
P.O. Box 5055
Fargo, ND 58105-5055
ndsu.nodak.edu

Ohio

Ohio Northern University (1, 2)
College of Pharmacy
Ada, OH 45810
onu.edu

Ohio State University (1, 2)
College of Pharmacy
500 W. Twelfth Ave.
Columbus, OH 43210-1291
acs.ohio-state.edu

University of Cincinnati (1, 2)
College of Pharmacy
P.O. Box 670004
Cincinnati, OH 45267-0004
uc.edu

University of Toledo (1, 2)
College of Pharmacy
2801 W. Bancroft St.
Toledo, OH 43606-3390
utoledo.edu

Oklahoma

Southwestern Oklahoma State University (1, 2)
School of Pharmacy
Weatherford, OK 73096
swosu.edu

University of Oklahoma (1, 2)
College of Pharmacy
P.O. Box 26901
Oklahoma City, OK 73190-5040
ou.edu

Oregon

Oregon State University (1)
College of Pharmacy
203 Pharmacy Building
Corvallis, OR 97331-3507
orst.edu

Pennsylvania

Duquesne University (1, 2)
Mylan School of Pharmacy
Pittsburgh, PA 15282-1504
duq.edu

Lake Erie College of Osteopathic Medicine (1)
School of Pharmacy
1858 W. Grandview Blvd.
Erie, PA 16509
lecom.edu

Philadelphia College of Pharmacy (1, 2)
School of Pharmacy
600 S. Forty-Third St.
Philadelphia, PA 19104-4495
usip.edu/academics/pharmacy

Temple University School of Pharmacy (1, 2)
3307 N. Broad St.
Philadelphia, PA 19140
temple.edu/pharmacy

University of Pittsburgh (1)
School of Pharmacy
3501 Terrace St.
Pittsburgh, PA 15261
pitt.edu

Wilkes University (1)
School of Pharmacy
P.O. Box 111
Wilkes-Barre, PA 18766
http://pharmacy.wilkes.edu

Puerto Rico

University of Puerto Rico (1)
School of Pharmacy
P.O. Box 365067
San Juan, PR 00936-5067
upr.clu.edu

Rhode Island

University of Rhode Island (1)
College of Pharmacy
41 Lower College Rd.
Kingston, RI 02881-0809
uri.edu

South Carolina

Medical University of South Carolina (1)
College of Pharmacy
P.O. Box 250141
Charleston, SC 29425-2301
musc.edu

University of South Carolina (1)
College of Pharmacy
Columbia, SC 29208
sc.edu

South Dakota

South Dakota State University (1, 2)
College of Pharmacy
P.O. Box 2202C
Brookings, SD 57007-0099
sdstate.edu

Tennessee

University of Tennessee (1, 2)
College of Pharmacy
847 Monroe Ave.
Memphis, TN 38163
tennessee.edu

Texas

Texas Southern University (1, 2)

College of Pharmacy and Health Sciences
3100 Cleburne St.
Houston, TX 77004
tsu.edu

Texas Tech University Health Sciences Center (1, 2)

School of Pharmacy
1300 S. Coulter St.
Amarillo, TX 79106
ttuhsc.edu

University of Houston (1, 2)

College of Pharmacy
4800 Calhoun Blvd.
Houston, TX 77204-5511
uh.edu

University of Texas at Austin (1, 2)

College of Pharmacy
Austin, TX 78712-1074
utexas.edu

Utah

University of Utah (1, 2)

College of Pharmacy
Salt Lake City, UT 84112
utah.edu

Virginia

Hampton University (1)
    School of Pharmacy
    Hampton, VA 23668
    hamptonu.edu

Medical College of Virginia (1, 2)
    School of Pharmacy/VCU
    410 N. Twelfth St.
    P.O. Box 980581
    Richmond, VA 23298-0581
    medschool.vcu.edu

Shenandoah University (1, 2)
    School of Pharmacy
    1460 University Dr.
    Winchester, VA 22601
    su.edu

Washington

University of Washington (1)
    School of Pharmacy
    H-364 Health Sciences Center
    P.O. Box 357631
    Seattle, WA 98195-7631
    washington.edu

Washington State University (1, 2)
    College of Pharmacy
    P.O. Box 646510
    Pullman, WA 99164-6510
    wsu.edu

West Virginia

West Virginia University (1, 2)
School of Pharmacy
P.O. Box 9500
Morgantown, WV 26506-9500
wvu.edu

Wisconsin

University of Wisconsin-Madison (1, 2)
Schools of Pharmacy
777 Highland Ave.
Madison, WI 53706
wisc.edu

Wyoming

University of Wyoming (1)
School of Pharmacy
P.O. Box 3375
Laramie, WY 82071-3375
uwyo.edu

About the Author

Fred B. Gable was associated with the faculty of Temple University School of Pharmacy for a period of twenty-five years, during which time he rose from the rank of instructor to full professor and assistant dean. Over this period he provided instruction in pharmacy courses to some three thousand students, and as director of admissions he recruited, counseled, and admitted every student who finally graduated during his tenure. Dean Gable applied for, received, and administered a multimillion-dollar government grant for the purpose of recruiting, retaining, and graduating disadvantaged students as pharmacists.

Over the years he served on national committees of the American Association of Collegiate Registrars and Admissions Officers, the American Association of Colleges of Pharmacy, and the American Pharmaceutical Association. While serving with the Medical Service Corps of the U.S. Army, his duties included assignments as evacuation hospital pharmacist, laboratory technician at Second

Army Area Laboratory, and assistant to the educational coordinator at Madigan Army Hospital, Tacoma, Washington.

Professor Gable is the author of papers published in *National Association of Retail Druggists Journal, American Druggist, American Journal of Pharmaceutical Education, The Apothecary, Proceedings of State Boards and Colleges of Pharmacy, Journal of the American Pharmaceutical Association* (Scientific Edition), *Journal of the American Pharmaceutical Association* (Practical Pharmacy Edition), and *The Pennsylvania Pharmacist*. He is author of *Psychosocial Pharmacy: The Synthetic Society* (Lea & Febiger), which deals with the role of pharmacy practitioners regarding such areas as child abuse, sexuality, contraception, and the terminal patient.

He is a member of the Society of Sigma Xi, Rho Chi Honor Society, Rho Pi Phi Fraternity, Phi Delta Chi Fraternity (honorary), Lambda Kappa Sigma Fraternity (honorary), Alpha Zeta Omega Fraternity (honorary), and is a life member of the Boards of Directors of the Pharmacy Alumni Association and the General Alumni Association of Temple University. Professor Gable's profile is included in the first edition of *Marquis Who's Who in Medicine and Healthcare, 1997–1998* and in the fifty-second edition of *Marquis Who's Who in America, 1998*.